SUPERINTEND WITH SUCCESS

By

GUY P. LEAVITT

Illustrated by

ROBERT E. HUFFMAN

THE STANDARD PUBLISHING COMPANY

Cincinnati, Ohio

3203

© MCMLX
THE STANDARD PUBLISHING COMPANY
Cincinnati, Ohio
Printed in U. S. A.

table of contents

Section I . . . YOU VISUALIZE

    Chapter 1—Your Job 9

Section II . . . YOU ORGANIZE

    Chapter 2—Your School as Part of the Church 20

    Chapter 3—Your School Into Departments and Grades 28

    Chapter 4—Your School's Teaching Materials and Curriculum 37

    Chapter 5—Your School's Program 44

Section III . . . YOU DEPUTIZE

    Chapter 6—Helpers 54

    Chapter 7—Officers 59

    Chapter 8—Teachers 69

    Chapter 9—By Training Officers and Teachers 75

    Chapter 10—By Rewarding Officers and Teachers 79

Section IV . . . YOU SUPERVISE

    Chapter 11—Yourself 88

    Chapter 12—Your Workers 97

    Chapter 13—Workers' Conferences 102

    Chapter 14—Pupils 107

    Chapter 15—Attendance 115

    Chapter 16—Equipment 123

    Chapter 17—Financing 132

Section V . . . YOU ANALYZE

    Chapter 18—Results 138

THE FOUR "IZES"

Business has what it calls the four "izes" of good management: Visual*ize*, Organ*ize*, Deput*ize*, and Superv*ise*. To these I have added a fifth: Anal*yze*.

The Sunday school is the biggest business on earth and produces the world's finest product—a Christian. The superintendent is called upon to employ these "izes." Hence, we have used them in heading up the sections of this book.

This business-like approach to the work of the superintendent accounts for the use of the second person, singular, in addressing him, and the charts, outlines, and other practical devices to avoid academic dryness and strive for readability. I want the superintendent to find this book to be enjoyable reading.

In it, I have summed up my own experiences and observations gained in half a century of serving in the Sunday school and of training others to serve. During that time I have learned all I know from thousands of successful superintendents and others who have been my teachers. To every one of them I am deeply grateful.

GUY P. LEAVITT
Holly Hill, Florida

Section 1

you visualize

Chapter 1—Your Job

    Learn the Purpose of the Sunday School

    Learn Why the Sunday School Is Important in the Work of Recruiting Christians

    Learn Why the Sunday School Is Important in the Work of Conserving Christians

    Learn the History of the Sunday School

    Learn Some Good Reasons for the Sunday School's Being for Adults as Well as Children

Can you name some reasons for the Sunday school's being an effective agent for recruiting people to Christ? Seven reasons are given on page 11.

What are the three major functions of the church? Find them on page 12.

Why is the Sunday school important to the work of conserving Christians? Read four reasons given on pages 12 and 13.

Do you know three basic motives that should prompt people to become workers in the Sunday school? They are listed on page 15.

What questions should you be able to answer as you attempt to understand the present effectiveness of your Sunday school? Page 17 contains some of these questions.

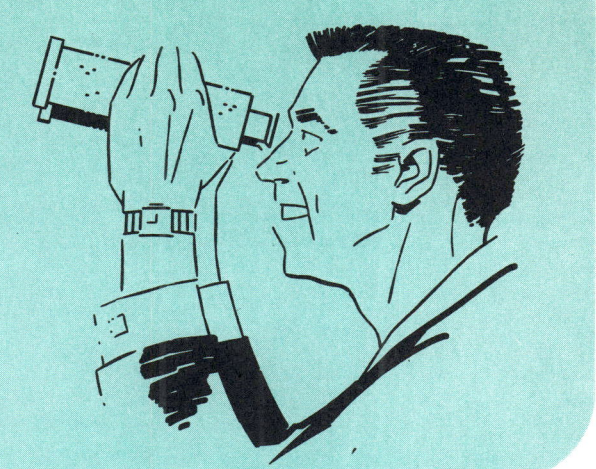

CHAPTER 1

YOU VISUALIZE

your job

To visualize one's job is to comprehend it, understand it, picture it in the mind. A superintendent must know what the Sunday school is supposed to do, why it is important. He also must know something about its past, present, and future.

The word "visualize" means to catch a vision, and "Where there is no vision, the people perish" the Bible tells us (Proverbs 29:18). What does this mean? The president of a multi-million-dollar corporation explained it to me this way: Three telephone men go out to repair three breaks in a line. One, who has no vision, merely repairs a wire that stretches from one telephone pole to another. The second, who has little vision, thinks of his job as repairing a wire that connects one town with another. The third, who has the real vision, and who enjoys his work to the utmost, visualizes himself as repairing a channel of communication that stretches around the world. Over those wires life and death of individuals and of nations may be determined; messages of happiness and of sorrow may be carried; the daily affairs of mankind may be transacted.

A superintendent who stops to visualize his job will ask, "Why is the Sunday school important?" Two grand facts testify to its importance. One has to do with the *Person* who is at the head of it. The other has to do with the *Purpose* of the Sunday school.

The *Person* is Jesus Christ, the Son of God, the head of the church —and the Sunday school is part of the church. Jesus is your chief. You work for Him. There can be no more important position in all the world than the one you hold as superintendent of a Sunday school, because of the Person for whom you work.

TEACH!

Your *purpose* is the most important any workman can have. It is to enlist and train people to be Christians. Others may enlist and train people for the armed forces, for factories, stores, schools, and farms; but their efforts are limited to this earth and to this life. You enlist and train people not only for life on this earth, but for eternity.

Let's look a little further into the two reasons that make your job as superintendent so important. Jesus Christ authorized your school. He, of course, is the Son of God, divine as no other individual who has walked the earth. He declared that all power or authority had been given to Him in heaven and in earth. Acting on this authority He then commanded: "Go . . . teach." That is what you and your school are doing. Your school is authorized by Christ, commissioned by Christ; and if it is the school that it ought to be, it is teaching the gospel message commanded by Christ.

What is your school teaching? Here, we come to the second purpose that makes your job so important: *the purpose of the school*. According to the Lord's plan this has two parts.

First, He said, "Go ye therefore, and teach all nations, baptizing them in the name of the Father, and of the Son, and of the Holy Ghost" (Matthew 28:19). The first part of your school's purpose, therefore, is to recruit people for Christ. You find them, bring them in, teach them, and baptize them. That is the first part of the job. But that isn't all of the job.

BAPTIZE!

After they are taught and baptized (recruited), there is more to be done. Jesus, being divine, and therefore perfect, knew this. He said that after we have recruited people for Him we are to continue "teaching them to observe all things whatsoever I have commanded you" (Matthew 28:20). This means that your school is not only to teach *what* He has commanded but that it is to lead people to observe, or to do, what He has said. This is called *conservation*, or development.

to live the abundant life daily!

* To summarize: Your school's purpose is to recruit people and teach them about Christ so that they will accept Him as their Lord and Master and will become members of His church. Then you are to teach them how to grow as Christians by doing what Christ has commanded.

TEACH!

Live!

THE WORK OF RECRUITING

For more than twenty years I wrote annually to ministers of churches that reported outstanding achievement in evangelism. I asked them to tell me what part their Sunday schools had in this success. The summary of the hundreds of reports received through the years was that at least three out of four additions to the church came through the Sunday schools. These same ministers testified that a higher percentage of converts secured through the Sunday school remains faithful than of those who do not come through the school. The Sunday school is the church at work, recruiting and conserving as the Lord commanded.

Several reasons can be given to explain why the Sunday school is so effective in recruiting people for Christ:

1. The Sunday school is the church's most productive source of prospects for church membership. Its list of pupils is carefully reviewed prior to any special evangelistic effort. In addition to non-church members who attend the Sunday school, the relatives, friends, and neighbors of Sunday-school pupils also are possible prospects.

2. Children are trained in the school. It is in childhood that most converts are gained. The late Walter S. Athearn's nationwide studies of the ages at which persons first become members of the Protestant churches in the United States showed that the median age of conversion is fourteen years, seven months, and fourteen days. The largest group falls in the thirteenth year, with one-fourth of the persons coming into the church under the age of eleven years, ten months, and twenty-two days. The figures reveal the startling fact that the chances are three to one that a person who has not become a member of the church by the time he or she reaches twenty-one *will never become a member*.

3. Every pupil is a recruiter; he brings others into the school and on into church membership.

4. The informality of the Sunday school appeals to the outsider and serves to introduce him to the more formal worship service, where he receives Christ as his Lord and Master.

5. The teacher, carrying out the Lord's command, faithfully leads the pupils into a saving knowledge and acceptance of His will. Someone has said that when it comes to winning souls to Christ in the Sunday school, the minister is across the street, the superintendent is at arm's length, but the teacher is face-to-face.

6. Many churches conduct a Sunday-school class in church membership. Some of these classes are held at special seasons, just prior to a concentrated effort in evangelism. Others are continuous and are for prospective members and church members who wish further instructions.

7. Individual pupils in Sunday school who are members of the church are encouraged to pray for those who are not yet church members. Thus the school recruits for Christ.

It is natural for the Sunday school to have a larger attendance than any other service of the church, for in the successful Sunday school are those who are being taught and led into church membership. The self-satisfied superintendent, who once boasted to me that every available member of his school was a member of the church, was unknowingly admitting failure. True, the *goal* is to win every member of the school for Christ, but in the successful school there are always newcomers, prospects for membership. The school's purpose is to recruit, to enlist, to "Go out into the highways and hedges" and seek and bring in the lost, that they may be saved.

They will not seek—*they must be sought*.

They will not come—*they must be brought*.

They will not learn *unless they are taught*.

THE WORK OF CONSERVATION

Having been recruited, or won to the church, the member must be conserved or developed as a Christian. The Lord's plan for His church provides for this conservation. According to His plan the member is developed in three ways:

1. *He is taught.* "Teaching them to observe all things whatsoever I have commanded you" (Matthew 28:20).

2. *He worships.* Repeatedly the Bible calls upon the believer to worship. "This do in remembrance of me" said Jesus (Luke 22:19), while in Hebrews 10:25 we are taught the necessity of "not forsaking the assembling of ourselves together."

3. *He serves.* Read Matthew 25:31-46 and many other passages.

The three major functions of the church, therefore, are these:

Teaching

Worshiping

Serving

The Sunday school joins in the functions of worship and service, but is not primarily responsible for those functions. It teaches their necessity and trains the individual in their practice. If the school, a department, or a class conducts a worship service, the purpose is to worship, to be sure; but the worship program in the school is not to take the place of the church's more formal program of worship. The school's purpose is to teach the importance of worship and the proper way to worship. Likewise, if the school, department, or class conducts a service project, such as collecting food for the poor, the purpose is not only to aid the poor but to teach the pupils the meaning and method of service. Such teaching is part of the work of conservation.

That the Sunday school is important in this part of the church's work is shown by the record. Church members who attend the Sunday school are almost always the church members who are active in the other work of the church. Those who come into the church by way of the Sunday school are more faithful in worship and service than those who come without benefit of Sunday-school training.

Several reasons may be given for your school's being so important in the work of conservation:

1. *The Sunday school puts the pupil to work.* "Use me or lose me" is the rule in the church as it is elsewhere. In the Sunday school even the newest pupil is encouraged to bring others. As he continues to attend and is given classroom responsibilities, he participates in programs, aids in projects, and becomes a worker in the church.

2. *It provides an encouraging fellowship.* The pupil becomes part of a group of his own age, having his own interests. The others in the group are his friends and fellow workers. If he is absent, they encourage him to return. If he suffers misfortune, they show concern. Led by the teacher, they encourage him to grow as a Christian.

3. *It teaches him the importance of worship and service as a Christian.* He is led to attend the worship services of the church and to serve in its work.

4. *It teaches him to give money*, as well as *time* and *talent*. He becomes an investor in the Lord's work, and therefore he is more interested in the work.

Jesus came to seek and to save the lost. The Sunday school's twin purposes are to seek the lost, and, having found them, to train them to do what Jesus has commanded. God's eternal plan is wrapped up in that simple statement. To conclude our brief look at the importance of your job as superintendent of a Sunday school, let me borrow (with their permission) from two writer friends of mine. First, from James DeForest Murch, in the *quod erat demonstrandum* set forth at the opening of his book, *Christian Education and the Local Church,* we read these words:

> If the gospel of Jesus Christ
> is the hope of the world—
> *And it is,*
> If the church is the divinely
> appointed agency for the dissemination
> of the gospel—
> *And it is,*
> If the church school is the recruiting
> station and training camp of
> the church—
> *And it is,*
> Then the church school is
> the hope of the world.

In his church paper, *The Fisherman,* M. Ralph Fisher, minister of Valley Forge Christian Church, Elizabethton, Tennessee, wrote this thought-provoking statement:

"Teaching God's Word is *not* an optional or extra-curricular activity of the church; it is the church's first and foremost duty. The saints of God will have the aeons of eternity for worshiping, but only the era of time for teaching. Bible school is, therefore, a present, pressing imperative."

The Sunday school is "big business," not only in regard to its purpose, but because of its present-day size. It is international in scope. Sunday schools are to be found in every land. The latest estimates at the time this is being written place the number of pupils in the United States Sunday schools alone at over four million, with between three and four hundred thousand officers and teachers. The cost of housing, maintaining, and operating these schools runs into hundreds of millions of dollars.

The importance of the Sunday school is also shown by its effect upon society. The millions of men and women who each week bring the teachings of the Holy Bible to its people are a nation's most valuable resource.

A learned speaker, according to the *New York Times*, told an International Sunday School Convention in Cleveland, Ohio, that the future of human freedom may depend on how good a job is done by the nation's Sunday schools. Our belief in the sacredness of human personality, he said, is a direct outgrowth of the Christian faith. If personality is not held sacred, then the state may well become supreme, as has been true throughout much of history, and liberty and justice will become mere words to be bandied about at the will of the dictator.

Through the years, American leaders have testified to the importance of the Sunday school.

Roger Babson, business statistician, speaking for the business world, said: "The Sunday school has tremendous opportunities. There never was a time in the history of our nation when the Sunday school was so much needed. It should be of especial interest to the young people. Only a spiritual awakening on the part of the young people of this world can prevent another great war. I especially appreciate the time and efforts of the teachers and other workers in the Sunday school. They are a noble lot."

J. Edgar Hoover, long-time director of the Federal Bureau of Investigation, United States Department of Justice, once said: "It is my belief that the Sunday school is of utmost importance in the training for citizenship. This early religious teaching is necessary if our young people are to contribute their full measure to the happiness and stability of the community when they are called upon to accept its responsibilities." Mr. Hoover, who has written many articles and made many speeches endorsing the Sunday school, is credited with saying, "Keep your child in Sunday school and you will keep him out of jail."

Another Hoover, the engineer-businessman President of the United States, declared that the Sunday school "is at the very root of the religious life, with all its benefits to the individual and the nation, and for this reason I cordially commend all efforts to enlarge its field of usefulness."

Such statements have been made and are being made by many great men of America. They agree that the Sunday school is vitally important to good citizenship, to the economic, social, and intellectual welfare of the nation.

Its importance to the church is the subject of the following article written by Don Earl Boatman of Ozark Bible College. Every superintendent will do well to read it when discouragement threatens. President Boatman wrote:

"The Bible school is a great factory where the raw material of human life is molded and fashioned and then brought along the assembly line to the Lord's Table and the inspiration of preaching and teaching at church that we may all grow in grace and in knowledge of God!

"What is the Bible school? The Bible school is the friend of childhood, the inspiration of youth, the strength of middle life, the comfort of declining years.

"It has God's day for its time, God's house for its place, God's book for its text, and God's glory for its aim.

"It is officered and taught by Christian men and women who are freely giving their time, talents, and tithes to the end that the lost may be saved and the saved may be strengthened.

"It builds character, instructs the mind, warms the heart, feeds ambition, encourages the faint-hearted, shields the tempted, and points the way of life for us all.

"It deserves the sympathetic support, the prayerful interests, the loyal co-operation of every loving Christian, of every patriotic citizen, and of every aspiring youth and prattling child.

"It stretches out a friendly hand to one and all, old or young, and bids them enter into the Father's house and listen to the Father's voice as He speaks forth out of His Holy Word.

"It directs the steps of men, women, and youth to the table of our Lord where we pause in church and remember that the just died for the unjust to bring us to God. Rarely do you find an overcrowded audience at the church and communion hour anywhere in this country unless there is also a crowded, spirit-filled Bible school."

This work of the Sunday school is not in the hands of well-paid, highly-trained and closely-supervised professionals; rather, it depends upon godly men and women who voluntarily undertake it from high and holy motives. These motives can be summed up as follows:

1. Love of Christ.
2. Desire to obey His commands.
3. Christian concern for others.

There can be no higher motives than these. To replace them with any other motive, such as earning a paycheck, is not to be considered. The voluntary nature of the Sunday school must be preserved. These workers recognize their limitations and realize there must be continuous effort toward improvement. They are heroically carrying the burden of the Sunday school and have a right to ask the church to help them by providing training and adequate supervision.

A GLANCE AT SUNDAY SCHOOL HISTORY

Teaching has been practiced in the church since its establishment in A.D. 30, and centuries before that God required it of His people, the Israelites. Acts 2:42 tells us that the first Christians continued steadfastly in teaching. The Christian church school, or Bible school, dates from that time. The Sunday school, however, began to gain prominence after a wealthy businessman, Robert Raikes, started such a school in Gloucester, England, in July, 1780. Prior to that time, as early as 1665 in Roxbury, Massachusetts, attempts had been made to hold Sunday schools in America. These early Sunday schools were not for one hour on Sunday morning, but began at eight o'clock in the morning and continued throughout the day, with time out for attending worship services.

An understanding of this bit of history will help to explain the various names given to the school:

Church school, for example, is a general term for all the teaching done by the church, including the Sunday morning school.

Bible school refers to the teaching of the Bible, whether in the home, church, or in weekday Bible classes conducted by a community.

Sunday school, however, has come to mean the class sessions on Sunday morning. A comprehensive term for the school would be the "Sunday morning Bible school of the church." You are the superintendent of the Sunday school—the period of instruction on Sunday morning.

A superintendent ought also to understand the changes that have come about in attitudes toward the Sunday school, its scope and importance. At first, in the Robert Raikes' school and until the early part of the present century, the school was for children only. Indeed, in the Raikes' school, the teaching was often done by the brighter children in the group. It was a school for children. Later, adults were paid to teach, and still later volunteer teachers were enlisted. Early in the nineteen hundreds, the Sunday schools began to expand to include older youth and adults. In the first quarter of this century, large classes of adults became popular.

There was good reason for this expansion. Adults need to learn from God's Word. No one ever learns all that the Scriptures have to teach. Also, it was discovered that young people were lost to the Sunday school, and often to the church, when their parents did not attend. The home, always considered important in Christian training, was more effective when all members of the family attended Sunday school. There is still the tendency in some churches to use the Sunday school for children only. The Sunday school is to be for all ages, since all ages need to learn about God's plan for us.

Attitudes toward the importance of the Sunday school have undergone change. At the beginning of the movement in England, the Archbishop of Canterbury called the bishops together to consider putting a stop to the Sunday schools. Wisdom prevailed, however, and Sunday schools were approved. In America, at first, opposition on the part of the church was vigorous. A young woman who attempted to hold a Sunday school for children in old First Church in Norwich Town, Connecticut, was denounced by the church authorities, who said her work was a desecration of the Lord's Day. Put out of the building, she and her pupils met regularly each week on the steps of the church building, and continued to do so until public sentiment demanded that they be readmitted.

In the early nineteen hundreds, when adult classes began to be popular, and Sunday-school attendance began to boom, another type of opposition was encountered. Some ministers and other church leaders, noticing a larger attendance at Sunday school than at the preaching service, denounced the school saying it was like "the tail wagging the dog," or it was "putting the cart before the horse." As the proper understanding of the Sunday school and its importance developed, however, this attitude changed. People no longer consider it to be separate from the church. They realize it is an important part of the church's program, as important as the preaching service or any other activity of the church. Every person needs to be present for worship and for study. No one should attend one and not the other.

A GLANCE AT YOUR OWN SCHOOL

Your concern, of course, is with your own school. It may be a good idea for you to review your school's history. When did it start? What have been its problems—its victories? Who have been its leaders? How successful were they? What caused them to succeed or to fail? To find the answers, review the school's records and visit with some "old timers" in the church.

How well do the workers in the school and the members of the church understand the purpose, importance, and scope of the Sunday school? Is your school organized as part of the church, by departments, with classes for all ages? How well trained are the officers and teachers? What methods are being used to supervise the school, its workers, pupils, equipment, finances, attendance, etc? You must be able to answer these questions if you are to know how your school is measuring up to the requirements for a good school!

When you understand how effective your school is now, you can begin to plan for its growth and improvement. Sunday-school methods are changing. The program of the past will not suffice today.

At one time people lived in the same neighborhood for generation after generation. Today one fifth of the entire population moves from one place to another every year. People formerly lived in downtown neighborhoods or on farms. Now they live in the suburbs of the cities. Even the farm is a suburb because of improved transportation and communications. The population is growing at a rate never before equaled. If the Sunday school is to keep up with these changes it must improve its organization, methods, and general effectiveness. Never before has the church had such an opportunity to teach as it has today.

Section 2

you organize

Chapter 2—Your School as Part of the Church

    What Is the Church?
    Your Part in the Church's Other Teaching Activities
    The Board of Christian Education
    The Superintendent and the Minister

Chapter 3—Your School into Departments and Grades

    Grading the Sunday School
    Your Departmental Workers
    Why Is Grading Necessary?
    How to Improve the Grading in Your School

Chapter 4—Your School's Teaching Materials or Curriculum

    The Uniform Lessons
    Group-graded Lessons
    Closely-graded Lessons
    Elective Courses

Chapter 5—Your School's Program

    The Annual Program
    The Sunday-morning Program

Can you define the church? What is the purpose of the church? Does it differ from the purpose of the Sunday school? Find the answers to these questions by reading pages 20 and 21 of this chapter.

Name some of the teaching activities of the church besides the Sunday school. Can you tell a little about each activity? Pages 22-24 will help you.

What are some of the tasks of the board of Christian education? Learn about them by reading page 25.

Do you know the seven suggestions for giving a good report to the board of education? They're listed on page 26.

Name some ways in which you and the minister or ministers can work together for a successful program. Page 27 will help you.

CHAPTER 2

YOU ORGANIZE

your school as part of the church

WHAT IS THE CHURCH?

Is the church a building? No, the church building may be "the church on the corner" to some people, but the church is not a building. Is it a service? No, the church is not an hour's service from 10:30 to 11:30 A.M. or 7:30 to 8:30 P.M. on Sunday.

What, then, is the church? The church is *people*—a particular or peculiar kind of people, but people. These people do many things. They worship, they sing, they pray, they study, they go about doing good, they work, and they play. They are the church just as much at a Sunday-school picnic as they are at a prayer meeting. They are the church just as much during the study hour on Sunday morning as they are at the worship service.

These people call themselves Christians because they have accepted Jesus Christ, the Son of God, as their leader. He is the head of the church. The church is His. His followers are different from other people because they strive to do what *He* wants them to do rather than what *they* want to do. They are the church now and always. This understanding of the church—who it is and what it is—will help us to know the place of the Sunday school in the church.

When the church began it did <u>three</u> basic things: It <u>taught</u> the Word of God, it <u>served</u> God and other people, it <u>worshiped</u> God. Today these are still the main functions of the church.

YOU ORGANIZE

Why does the church teach? Why does it serve? Why does it worship? Or, in other words, what is the purpose of the church? The purpose of the church is identical with that of the Sunday school, for the Sunday school is part of the church. That purpose is <u>to recruit people to the army of Christians</u> <u>under the leadership of Christ</u>, and <u>to train them in the Christian life</u>. As superintendent of the Sunday school you serve as head of this important part of the church.

The superintendent of the Sunday school is an officer of the church and is elected by the congregation. He reports to the board or committee of Christian education, which has charge of <u>all educational activities of the church</u>. He is co-worker with the minister and with the chairmen of the youth work, women's work, men's work, etc. He is an important member of an important team.

In a real sense the superintendent is a minister of Christ. Although he reports to the board of Christian education, he is responsible to Christ. He may not be paid a salary by the local church, but he is on the "pay roll" of the Lord, and has the promise of being richly rewarded. He must succeed. He dare not fail.

The church has a program, usually planned by the leaders of its various activities, to enable it to accomplish its purpose. This program includes <u>teaching</u>, <u>preaching</u>, <u>missions</u>, <u>stewardship</u>, <u>benevolence</u>, etc. As a member of the church and superintendent of the Sunday school, you must be fully acquainted with this program and must lead the school in co-operating with the whole church in accomplishing the program. Indeed, you will help plan the program.

Suppose the church is planning to conduct a special campaign to recruit new people for Christ. You can see to it that the Sunday school furnishes the names and addresses of people on its rolls who are not members of the church. You can also help by sending out Sunday-school teachers and workers to call on prospective members, urging teachers to emphasize the importance of becoming a Christian, and boosting attendance at the evangelistic preaching services.

The Sunday school can help in similar ways to promote stewardship, interest in missions, or a building project. The Sunday school plays an important role in every campaign and activity of the church. This fact is further illustrated below:

1. The church's purpose is to <u>recruit</u> for Christ. The Sunday school, as part of the church, is its most effective recruiting agent.
2. The church must <u>conserve each recruit</u> by enlisting and training him in the Lord's work. Again, the Sunday school takes the lead in this activity.
3. Worship is a primary function of the church. The Sunday school <u>teaches</u> the importance of <u>worship</u> and leads each pupil <u>to participate</u> in the general worship program of the church.
4. Service to God and others is an important part of the Lord's teaching. The Sunday school takes part in <u>ministering to the poor</u> and <u>needy</u>, those <u>who are sick</u>, and those <u>who are in prison</u>.

YOUR PART IN THE CHURCH'S OTHER TEACHING ACTIVITIES

The term "church school" applies to all the teaching activities of the church. When we say "Christian education and the local church" we refer to all the teaching activities of the church, not simply to the Sunday-morning school. These other activities are important to your school because the one-hour periods on Sunday morning are not adequate for thorough Christian training.

Included in these other teaching activities are the worship services, Sunday-evening training groups, vacation Bible school, week-day education (in day schools or in released-time classes from the public schools), summer camps, midweek classes, Christian education in the home, etc.

What have you, the superintendent of the Sunday school, to do with these activities? You and your school are to co-operate with all of them. How? Let us consider each of these activities briefly and discuss how you can help each one to succeed.

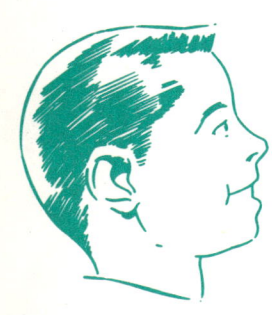

Worship services. Most churches follow the Sunday-morning plan of having a study period followed by a worship service, or vice versa. Other churches departmentalize the worship period just as they do the study period. This means that there are separate services for pre-school boys and girls, Primary children, Juniors, and young people and adults. Sometimes, when space is limited, the services may be duplicated, with one group worshiping while the other studies.

Whatever plan is adopted, the Sunday school is to give full co-operation. It is just as bad for pupils to go home after the study period and not remain for worship as it is to attend worship without being present for study. Every person needs both if he is to grow as a Christian. Your school can help in these ways:

1. Provide classes for all ages, so that parents can both study and worship. If the parents are there, the children will be there too.

2. Encourage separate worship services for the children so that they will enjoy and profit by the entire Sunday-morning program.

3. Teach and emphasize the fact that every individual needs to study *and* worship.

4. Include attendance at worship services in grading your pupils every Sunday morning.

5. See to it that every member of your faculty and staff attends the worship service.

6. Urge the minister and church officers to take an active part in the Sunday school.

Sunday-evening training groups. These groups may be for young people only, or for people of all ages. They may be called training groups, Christian Endeavor societies, fellowships, youth groups, etc. Their purpose is the same as that of the church and Sunday school.

But just as the Sunday school is perhaps most effective in bringing people to Christ, the training groups are most effective in training people to serve and thus to grow as Christians. Nearly everyone who becomes a preacher, missionary, or other specialized church worker has been active in this type of group.

The Sunday school should encourage every member to attend the Sunday-evening classes. Perhaps the weekly grading of the pupils can include training group attendance just as it includes attendance at worship services. Each teacher can emphasize to her class the importance of these training groups.

Vacation Bible school is usually conducted by the church on weekdays, for a period of one or two weeks during the summer. Most churches select the weeks immediately following the spring dismissal of public school. The pupils may range in age from three to the early teens. Vacation Bible school classes meet in the church buildings and on the church grounds. They are taught by adults who are members of the church. The Christian education committee selects the curriculum which is paid for from the church treasury.

Because they are so closely related, the vacation Bible school is occasionally sponsored by the Sunday school. Almost always the teachers and helpers are from the Sunday-school faculty, and most of the pupils are members of the Sunday school.

The vacation Bible school is very important because of the extra time it affords for Christian education. Sunday-school pupils who attend vacation school are usually far more advanced in Biblical studies than those who do not attend. Every effort should be made, therefore, to have every Sunday-school child in vacation Bible school and to provide the best possible teachers and helpers.

Weekday Christian education was growing rapidly in popularity until a few years ago when the courts decided that Bible teaching by public-school teachers in public-school property was unconstitutional because it violated the principle of separation of church and state. This did not interfere, however, with the practice of granting public-school pupils released time from the schoolroom to attend Bible classes away from the school grounds, taught by teachers not in public pay.

Churches sometimes conduct after-school classes with considerable success. Saturday-morning classes are also popular with some churches. A few congregations sponsor and operate their own Christian day schools. In such schools, secular subjects, as well as Biblical, are taught by Christian teachers. Here again, the Sunday school can do much to arouse and maintain interest in and support of the weekday classes.

Summer camps are attended almost entirely by pupils from the Sunday school. These Christian service camps, as they are sometimes called, help young people to understand the meaning of living for Christ and to appreciate Christian fellowship. Many of those who devote their lives to specialized service in the church have received their challenge and inspiration in summer camps.

In addition to the encouragement that the Sunday school gives each pupil to attend camp, it often pays part or all the expenses of every person who wishes to go.

Midweek classes, springing from the historic prayer meeting, offer another opportunity for Christian education. There should be classes for children as well as young people and adults. This midweek hour is an excellent time to combine teaching with devotional worship. Needless to say, all Sunday-school workers should attend. Occasionally the hour of devotion and study may be followed by a Sunday-school staff meeting at which the problems and plans of the Sunday school are discussed.

During the midweek sessions a particular book of the Bible may be studied. Such subjects as the life of Christ, the life of Paul, church history can be both interesting and valuable to Sunday-school workers and pupils. Whatever studies are used, they must be graded to fit the needs of each class or group.

Christian education in the home. The home was God's first school. In Deuteronomy 6:5-9, 2 Timothy 1:5, and elsewhere in the Scriptures the importance of teaching God's Word in the home is emphasized.

Members of a family receive Christian education in their home when they prepare and study their Bible-school lessons in advance, have devotions each day with Bible reading and prayer, read Sunday-school take-home papers together, etc. The Sunday school helps to bind the home and the church together. Its teachers call in the homes of the pupils. They urge families to attend services of the church as complete units. The Sunday school holds socials. These may be class parties, departmental "get-togethers," pot-luck suppers for the entire Sunday school. The Sunday school takes advantage of weddings, funerals, birthdays, anniversaries, etc., to help the families in the church. Some churches hold parent-teacher meetings so that families can become better acquainted with the purpose and workings of the Sunday school.

There are many other teaching activities of the church that could be mentioned such as the Boy Scouts and Girl Scouts, church-sponsored sports, choirs, youth rallies, conferences, the cradle roll, church extension department (for the purpose of ministering to people who cannot attend Sunday school, either because of illness or working hours). The Sunday school can and must help to make all these activities successful.

THE BOARD OF CHRISTIAN EDUCATION

To co-ordinate and direct the teaching activities of the church there should be a board of Christian education. This board may be made up entirely or partially of the elders in the church because they are responsible for overseeing the congregation, making sure that all teachings are true to the Bible, and working toward the success of the church program.

The superintendent is selected by this board, and recommended to the congregation for its approval. Usually he is elected for a one-year term. Since there is much to learn in order to be a successful superintendent, and since experience is the best training, the superintendent is returned to office year after year, but only so long as he is the person best qualified for the job. When the school ceases to thrive under his leadership, the annual election offers a convenient opportunity for the change.

In many schools the superintendent is an elder. This is desirable, however, only when an elder is the person best qualified to be superintendent. Sometimes a woman or even a young person makes the best superintendent available.

The one-year term in office is good also for teachers and other Sunday-school staff members. It provides opportunity for ineffective workers to be replaced with more capable ones. Of course extreme care should be taken before such replacements are made. Personalities are involved, and the work may be harmed by rashness.

The teachers are chosen by the board of education, but in their selection and acceptance, the line of organization is to be followed! Here is a good method: the superintendent, in conference with the board of education, the minister, and director of education (if there is one) select capable people to be leaders in the various departments of the Sunday school. Each leader is then called to help select the teachers for his particular department. When the teachers are selected each leader becomes responsible for the faculty in his department. Each department leader contacts each of his teachers, offering her the position, describing the duties involved, and gaining her acceptance or rejection. The leader then reports the result of each contact to the general superintendent who in turn reports it to the board of education.

The board of Christian education also selects the curriculum for the school. Again, the superintendent, minister, and others will probably help make the selection. The selection is limited to general policy and oversight since every lesson cannot be individually studied and reviewed. When the superintendent knows what type of curriculum is to be used he consults with the departmental leaders and their teachers who select specific quarterlies and teaching aids. These materials are then ordered, received, and distributed by the Sunday-school librarian.

In a general way, the board of education supervises the school's program of activities. The superintendent and his fellow workers plan a program and explain it to the board. The board approves, rejects, or alters the program. Then it is up to the superintendent to carry out his plans.

As superintendent, you will submit reports, at least once a year, to the board of Christian education, or to the entire congregation. These reports should be written. Here are some suggestions for making them effective:

1. *Give the facts.* Be a good reporter, making sure the "five W's" of newspaper reporting—what, who, when, where, why—are included.

2. *Be brief* when making recommendations. "Long-windedness" can be fatal.

3. *Organize your report* well, beginning with new and significant developments.

4. *Use simple language,* making every word count. Wordy reports are dull, uninteresting, and ineffective.

5. *Use graphs, charts, and objects* to help present your report more clearly.

6. *Tell of your decisions and give opinions,* but be sure you have the facts to back them up. Sometimes you must offer several possible solutions to a problem and let the others help decide which is best.

7. *Keep everyone concerned fully informed about your work.* Give oral reports and written reports to groups and individuals in addition to the formal annual report. Be sure that no one is ignorant of the progress, problems, and plans of the Sunday school.

THE SUPERINTENDENT AND THE MINISTER

No doubt your church has a minister. Perhaps it also has an associate minister, a minister of music, a youth director, and a minister of Christian education. You, the superintendent of the Sunday school, are closely connected with the minister or ministers.

You are a volunteer, unsalaried, and to a considerable extent, untrained in your work. The minister has been formally educated for his position and earns his living by his work. You are working with the church as a whole, but your primary responsibility is the Sunday-morning school. The minister also works with the church as a whole; he has many responsibilities in addition to the Sunday school. For example, he is as much responsible for the worship service as for the teaching service. He is as concerned about the training classes on Sunday evening as he is about the school on Sunday morning. He realizes, however, that the success of his ministry depends more upon the success of the Sunday school than on any other single activity of the church. Therefore, he is greatly interested in your work and is eager to do all he can to promote it.

The associate minister has been similarly educated and is also interested in the Sunday school. In fact, he may be able to give more of his time to work with you and the school than would the minister.

The minister of music is interested in your school as a source of members for his choirs. He probably considers music to be more important in the worship than in the teaching program of the church, but he realizes its educational values. He can work with you in many ways.

Of course the minister of Christian education is directly interested in your school. He works with all the teaching activities of the church, but especially with the school, for it is the largest and most important.

YOU ORGANIZE

The youth director gives chief attention to the young people's activities. These include the Sunday school's youth departments.

Your relationship with the minister is vitally important to the work of the church. How do you work together? Do you practice the following suggestions?

1. Remember that a minister is educated and experienced. He has dedicated his life to specialized service to the Lord you serve. He knows the importance of your school and wants it to succeed.

2. Confer with him personally and seek his advice.

3. Invite him to attend and take part in all workers' conferences.

4. Help him to hold any position in the school that he desires.

5. Keep well informed of the minister's program of activity and lead your school in helping to make it a success.

You and your school can help in these and other ways to make the work of the minister a success. What can you, in turn, expect of the minister? How can he help you and the Sunday school?

1. You have a right to expect the minister to show an interest in the Sunday school.

2. You can expect him to publicize the Sunday school.

3. The minister ought to work closely with the school by attending conferences, talking with the superintendent, and working with the board of education.

4. He can give suggestions for the selection of teachers.

5. He should aid in selecting the curriculum for the school.

Your work with the minister or ministers of the church may vary in detail, but in a general way it is the same. The minister, whether as evangelist, associate, director of music, youth director, or minister of education, can help you and your school; and you can help him to have a successful work. You are to be a team under the leadership of Jesus Christ.

The Sunday school always has been and probably always will be staffed by volunteers. You and your fellow workers undertake your work from such high and holy motives as love for Christ and His church, love and concern for your fellowmen and for the lost. You are not formally educated for the work. You know that you need the close supervision of technically trained and salaried leaders such as ministers. This means that there must be teamwork of the highest order—Christian teamwork—if the job is to be done.

Do you know some of the grading plans for schools of various sizes? Study the chart on page 30 to become familiar with these plans.

How should a Sunday-school teacher be selected? You will find the correct procedure reviewed on page 31.

Can you name four reasons why grading the Sunday school is important? They are given for you on page 32.

Give the "key words" to the general characteristics of pupils in each age group. You will find these words in the charted outline on pages 33 and 34.

What four basic rules will help you in grading your school? Read and study these rules which are given on page 36.

CHAPTER 3

YOU ORGANIZE

your school into departments and grades

Your Sunday school is graded, just as all human society is graded, according to development. "When I was a child," said the apostle Paul, "I spake as a child, I understood as a child, I taught as a child: but when I became a man, I put away childish things" (1 Corinthians 13:11).

The organization for Christian education has no complete blueprint in the New Testament. The Lord has not told us to teach according to a graded plan. He has left this to our common sense, merely admonishing us through the words of the apostle Paul, "Let all things be done decently and in order" (1 Corinthians 14:40). His church is to teach, and if it teaches effectively, the teaching must be done so that the pupil can understand and apply the teaching to his own life. This means teaching by grades—graded teaching.

Pupils below school age are classed according to their ages as are pupils who have graduated from high school. But pupils who attend public school are grouped according to their public-school grades. Some schools also divide classes by sexes—boys in one, girls in another. This is not recommended. Children are not separated in the public school, so separating them in Sunday school may cause them to look upon it as an odd and unnatural institution. As the pupils grow older and choose an elective course such as "Christian Courtship and Marriage," or when there is a demand for a class of men or a class of women, separation by sex may be desirable. For children, however, mixed classes are better. [Many authorities, however, insist that Juniors,

YOU ORGANIZE

especially, can be taught better if the sexes are separated. It is true that the Junior age is the age of sex antagonism. Also, there are many interesting things that can be done with the classrooms and with class socials if the sexes are separated. Actually the Juniors can be taught successfully either way.]

The following discussion of grading and the chart on page 30 give the generally accepted plans for Sunday-school organization. The superintendent should know these plans as well as he knows the alphabet. It is his Sunday-school chart and compass.

First in grading come the divisions in the school. There are three basic divisions: children—birth through sixth grade; youth—seventh grade through twenty years of age; and adults. These divisions exist in all schools, whether large or small. In very small schools having an attendance of fifteen or twenty there is one class for each division.

As a school grows in numbers, more classes are added, with several classes in each division. Each division may be a department with a person other than a teacher acting as departmental superintendent:

Children's Department under one superintendent
{
Cradle Roll, birth to 2 years
Nursery Class, ages 2 and 3
Kindergarten Class, ages 4 and 5
Primary Class, grades 1, 2, and 3
Junior Class, grades 4, 5, and 6
}

(Please notice that the name "Kindergarten" is used instead of "Beginner" because the pupil is not a beginner if he has attended the school's Nursery Class.)

Youth Department under a special superintendent
{
Junior High, grades 7, 8, 9
High School, grades 10, 11, 12
Young People, College students or ages 18-20
}

Adult Department consists of people from twenty-one years of age on up. In some schools the Young People's Department includes ages up to twenty-five. The Adult Department is also under a special superintendent.

Larger schools are divided further into more departments and classes. The chart on page 30 shows you how. Study Plan III and Plan IV carefully. In very large schools there may be not only several classes of one age group, but several departments, with a special superintendent for each. In such cases a supervisor may be appointed over several departments of one age group. All superintendents under him report to him. He in turn reports to the general superintendent.

How many classes should be in a department? What should be the maximum number of pupils in a class? The answers depend upon the ages of the pupils, the skill of the teacher, and the classroom space available. A good general rule to follow is this: the more departments and classes you can provide with a minimum number of pupils in each class, the more effective the teaching will be.

GRADING PLANS FOR SCHOOLS OF VARIOUS SIZES

Plan I—In the smallest schools there are pupils in each division with a teacher for each group. Each division, therefore, is a department. Each teacher is a departmental superintendent and reports to the general superintendent of the school.

Plan II—In somewhat larger Sunday schools the Cradle Roll and Home Departments are added. Classes are divided into six groups. The double underlines show that certain classes come under one department. In this plan six departmental superintendents are needed. Some teachers may also serve as superintendents of their departments.

Plan III—For a still larger school even more classes and departments are needed, with superintendents who are *not* teachers. There may be several classes in each department: two Nursery, two Kindergarten, three Primary classes, etc.

Plan IV—A large, closely-graded school has one or more classes for each age group. The departments are headed by superintendents who are not teachers. Therefore, at least twelve departmental superintendents are needed.

GENERAL SUPERINTENDENT

PLAN I — DIVISIONAL SUPERINTENDENTS

CHILDREN	YOUNG PEOPLE	ADULTS
Birth Through Grade 6	Grade 7 to 20 Years	21 Years and Up

PLAN II — DEPARTMENTAL SUPERINTENDENTS

PRE-SCHOOL		PRIMARY	JUNIOR	YOUNG PEOPLE		ADULTS	HOME DEPT.
CRADLE ROLL	NURSERY & KINDER.	PRIMARY	JUNIOR	JUNIOR HIGH	HIGH SCHOOL	ADULTS	HOME DEPT.

PLAN III — DEPARTMENTAL SUPERINTENDENTS

CRADLE ROLL	NURSERY	KINDER- GARTEN	PRIMARY	JUNIOR	JUNIOR HIGH	HIGH SCHOOL	OLDER YOUTH	YOUNG ADULTS	ADULTS	HOME DEPT.

PLAN IV — DEPARTMENTAL SUPERINTENDENTS

Cradle Roll	Nursery	Kind.	Primary	Junior	Jr. High	High School	Older Youth	Young Adults	Middle Adults	Older Adults	Home Dept.
BIRTH TO 2 YEARS	2 YR. OLDS / 3 YR. OLDS	4 YEARS / 5 YEARS	1st GRADE / 2nd GRADE / 3rd GRADE	4th GRADE / 5th GRADE / 6th GRADE	7th GRADE / 8th GRADE / 9th GRADE	10th GRADE / 11th GRADE / 12th GRADE	AGES 18-24 as many classes as needed	AGES 25-34	AGES 35-64	AGES 65 ON UP	ALL PEOPLE WHO CANNOT ATTEND S.S.

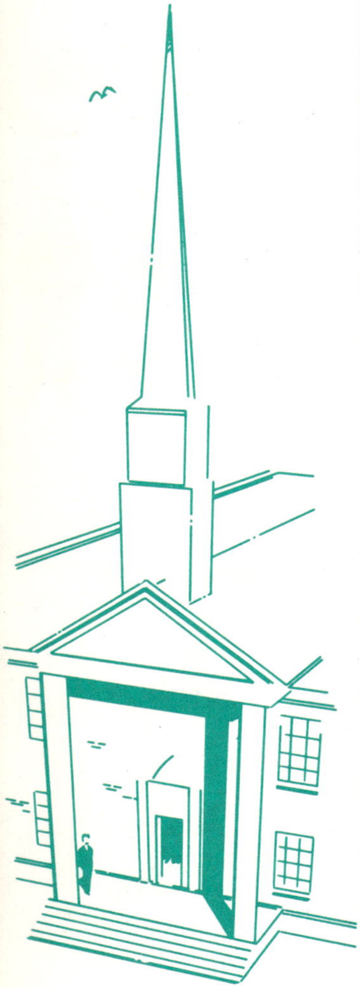

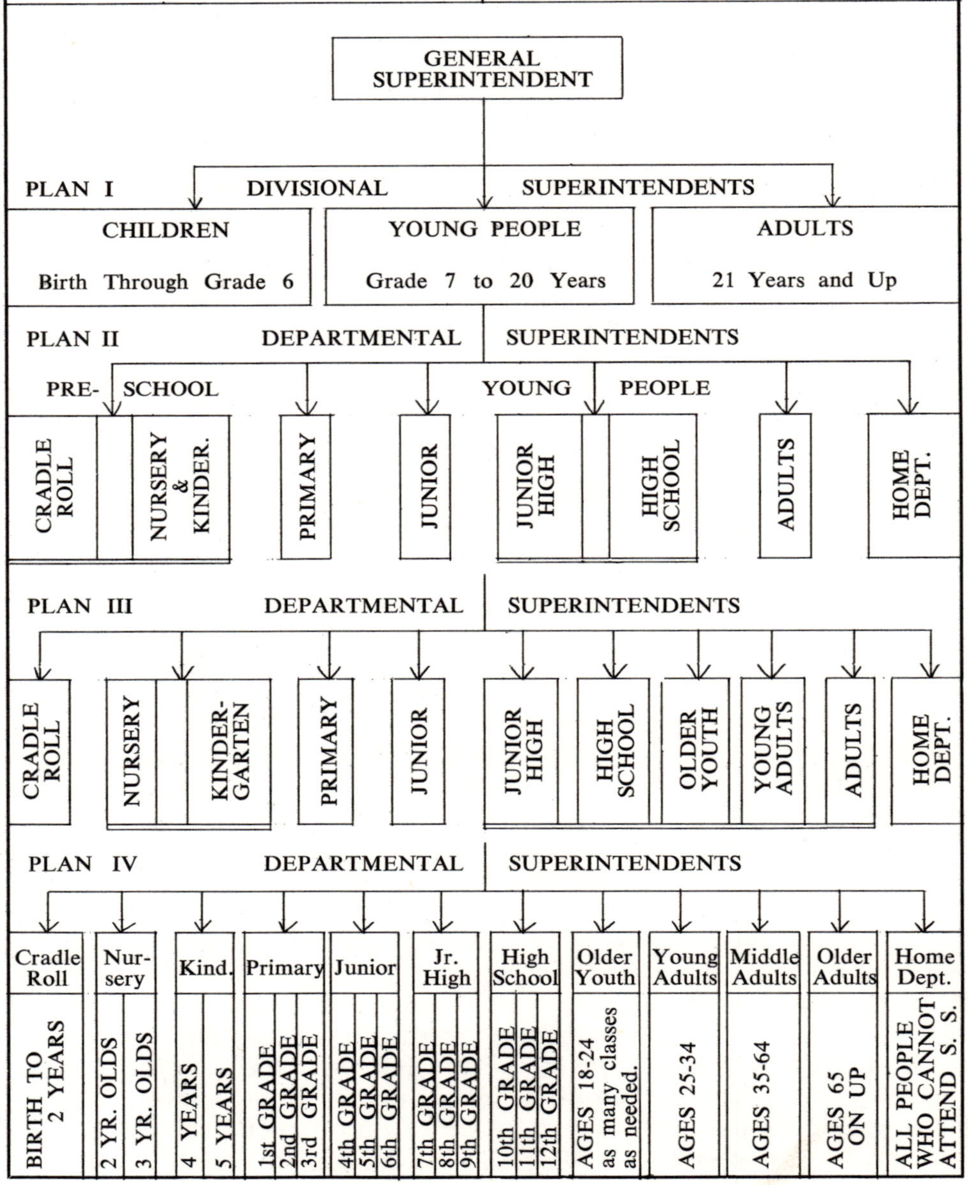

YOU ORGANIZE

YOUR DEPARTMENTAL WORKERS

Each department has as its head a "superintendent" or "principal" who works under you, the general superintendent. In a small school having only one class in each department, each teacher is also a departmental superintendent. In a school which has only two or three classes in each department, the more experienced, or the most capable teacher of each department can serve also as superintendent.

Under these departmental superintendents are the teachers in their departments and such other workers as are needed. These other workers may include assistant superintendents and teachers, secretaries, pianists, and librarians.

The general superintendent keeps in close touch with the departmental superintendents and workers. All of them attend his meetings of teachers and officers and take active parts in the work of the school as a whole.

As the school grows in number, the departments function apart from one another more and more. They hold all of their Sunday-morning sessions separately. Their teachers and workers hold their own staff meetings or conferences, conducted by their own departmental superintendents.

Always, however, the general superintendent is at the head of the Sunday-morning school, no matter how large it is. The departmental superintendents report to him. He talks with them about the plans and problems of their departments. He is responsible for them, and for the entire school, in the eyes of the board of Christian education.

In your dealings with the departmental superintendents, you must be careful to follow the line of organization. Do not "go over their heads" in matters concerning the workers or pupils in various departments.

Do you remember how a teacher or an associate teacher is to be selected? The departmental superintendent reports any pending vacancy to you. You, with this departmental worker, and perhaps with the minister and a member of the board of education of your church, discuss possible candidates for the position. You select one or more who are suitable. You then go before the entire board of Christian education, report the vacancy, and recommend one or more candidates. The board, after careful consideration, makes a selection and reports its decision to you. You, the general superintendent, do *not* notify the candidate. Instead, you tell the departmental superintendent of the board's selection. He or she is to supervise the work of the new appointee! Thus, the departmental superintendent should be the one to notify the new teacher about the appointment, give instructions regarding the position, and direct the work. This is the very important line-of-organization method used in businesses, public schools, and factories. When a general superintendent by-passes the departmental superintendent, the result can be disastrous. Self-confidence can be destroyed,

the importance of the job taken away, and the organization of the school upset. Teamwork is essential to the success of the school. This teamwork is possible only when each member of the team is given the responsibility that goes with his position.

Each departmental superintendent, under your supervision, organizes and directs the program in his or her department, keeps its records, distributes its literature and supplies, maintains discipline, promotes attendance, and conducts the department as a unit of the school. You and your program are to be the unifying influence that ties the departments together and keeps them functioning as a school. No one department is more important than another. You must treat them all alike. You are responsible for the success of all of them.

WHY IS GRADING NECESSARY?

Grading is necessary because no two age groups are alike. They differ in vocabulary, in understanding based upon experience and observation, in their behavior, and in their interests. A baby may be placed in a class of three-year-olds, but he will not learn and his presence will interfere with the learning of the others. A child may be put into a class of young people, or a young person into a class of adults, and the results will be the same. The younger pupil will not learn as he should, and the teacher's effort to include him in the instruction will hinder the older pupils.

These sharp distinctions lessen with age. There is a far wider gap between children of three and four, or four and five, than there is between adults of thirty and forty, or forty and fifty.

Grading is necessary if the pupil is to learn. This is true in the public school and it is true in the Sunday school. Even in the old-time, one-room public school, there were classes for each age group. The third-graders, for example, could not be put into a spelling class or arithmetic class with the fifth-graders without hampering the progress of pupils in both grades.

Grading is necessary if the teacher is to do her best teaching. Some teachers understand children and delight in teaching them, but would hesitate to try to teach adults. Other teachers are trained to teach adults, but do not know how to teach children. Both groups of teachers may have mastered the sciences of pedagogy and theology, but they may be miles apart in their knowledge of pupil psychology, one knowing how to deal with the child's mind, the other able to understand adults.

Grading is necessary if Sunday-school literature is to be used to the best advantage. Just as a second-grade pupil in public school would gain nothing from studying a seventh-grade text book, a Primary pupil in Sunday school would learn little or nothing if he were taught from a Junior High manual. Sunday-school literature has been published for all ages. Each teacher's manual, pupil's book, and "take-home" paper has been carefully prepared for a specific age or department. Only if the Sunday school is graded, with each teacher using

YOU ORGANIZE

the teaching materials prepared especially for his class, can Sunday-school literature be used to the best advantage.

Grading is also used in regard to chairs, tables, and other furniture, songs, programs, pictures on the walls, and anything else that will aid the pupil in receiving a Christian education. The more careful your Sunday school is with its grading, the better work it will be able to do.

As superintendent, you are not expected to know in detail the capabilities and characteristics of pupils of various ages. You do not deal directly with the pupils. The teachers and superintendents in the various departments are specialists in their age groups. That is one reason for your working with the departmental superintendents and not with the pupils personally. However, you will want to have a general knowledge of the characteristics of each age group and the aim that each teacher is striving for. The charted outline on this page and the next will help you to learn these things.

PERIOD IN LIFE	GENERAL CHARACTERISTICS	TEACHER'S AIM
I. INFANCY *Cradle Roll* (Years 0, 1)	KEY WORD: *Discovery* Physical—active, growing rapidly Mental—sees everything, wants to handle Spiritual—all he does is determined by others.	To give right responses (Exodus 2:9)
II. CHILDHOOD *Nursery Class* (Years 2 and 3)	KEY WORD: *Imitation* Physical—active, leisurely, "me do it" Mental—realistic, inquisitive, likes "touch and feel" Spiritual—likes regular prayer before meals and bedtime; meaning of "Thank you, God" is clearer.	To impress (Mark 10:14)
Kindergarten (Years 4 and 5)	KEY WORD: *Receptivity* Physical—continual motion, restless, wiggler Mental—open mind, a bundle of questions Spiritual—credulous, trusting, literal.	To guide (Psalm 32:8)
Primary (Grades 1, 2, 3)	KEY WORD: *Activity* Physical—active, play is important Mental—curious, imaginative, wants certainty Spiritual—discerning, capacity for reverence.	To control (Proverbs 22:6)
Junior (Grades 4, 5, 6)	KEY WORD: *Energy* Physical—unbounded energy, loud, boisterous, thoughtless Mental—retentive memory, hero worshiper, inquisitive Spiritual—Worshiper, "doer of the Word"	To direct (2 Timothy 3:15)

PERIOD IN LIFE	GENERAL CHARACTERISTICS	TEACHER'S AIM
III. YOUTH *Junior High* (Grades 7, 8, 9)	KEY WORD: *Transition* Physical—rapid change, awkward Mental—critical, self-reliant, self-important, emotional Spiritual—religious awakening, faith yielding to reason, "Why, why!"	To establish comradeship (1 Kings 20:40)
High School (Grades 10, 11, 12)	KEY WORD: *Aspiration* Physical—loves achievement, emerging into manhood and womanhood Mental—radical, extreme, doubting Spiritual—unstable, age of decisions.	To train (Ecclesiastes 12:1)
College Age (Years 18 - 25)	KEY WORD: *Self-assurance* Physical—Mature Mental—real thinkers, reason and judgment Spiritual—earnest seeking, sometimes scoffing.	To challenge (1 Timothy 4:12)
IV. ADULT *Early Maturity* (Years 25 - 34)	KEY WORD: *Application* A general getting down to business; definite tasks are begun and definite goals chosen.	To test (Hebrews 12:1)
Full Maturity (Years 35 - 64)	KEY WORD: *Achievement* Life is fully launched; each individual is himself, a settled state.	To co-operate (1 Peter 5:3)
Late Maturity (Years 65 and up)	KEY WORD: *Meditation* Decrease in bodily strength. Good, experienced judgment and knowledge; decreased social interest. Need activities to forget self; sense of being needed; faith in life to come.	To honor (2 Timothy 4:8)

HOW TO IMPROVE THE GRADING IN YOUR SCHOOL

Do not feel bad if your school is not correctly graded in its departments, lessons, program, and equipment. Ever since the modern Sunday-school movement began, grading has been a problem. It still is. One reason is that the Sunday school is manned by volunteers, and these workers often are not informed regarding the principles of grading. Another reason is that grading itself is continually being changed. For example, leaders disagree concerning the ages that are to be included in the Primary Department. In fact, they do not all agree that it is to be *called* the Primary Department. Age groupings, names of the groups, and methods of dealing with age groups are continually changing.

Everyone agrees, however, on the importance of grading. Your school, in order to do its best work, must be graded. The ages covered by the different groups and the names you give the groups are not as important as the fact that your school needs to be graded. In grading your school you will want to follow as closely as possible the accepted age groupings and names.

How you grade the Sunday school will depend to some extent upon the size of the school, the classrooms, and the number of capable teachers. Perhaps yours is a very small school, meeting in only one room. Or it may be a large school, meeting in a well-equipped educational unit. The size of the school will help to determine your program of grading.

Another thing to consider is whether or not the present teaching staff is trained to do graded work. You may have more teachers who can teach adults than you need and too few who can teach children.

One thing is almost certain: your school has a grading problem. Growing schools usually do. You cannot establish classes and departments and then forget about grading. The situation is always changing. The need for new classes may bring about a shift in classrooms, additions to the teaching staff, and changes in departmental leaders and workers.

You may also have a problem of arrangement. Do the classes in each department meet separately from the classes in the other departments? Are the classes in each department meeting together in one section of the building, or are they scattered? In one school the adult classes occupied two lovely rooms, while the children were crowded into nooks and corners. The adult classes had spent money to beautify their rooms and were justly proud of them. But the superintendent realized that the large adult classes had to be divided and assigned to smaller rooms so that the children's departments could function properly.

Sometimes teachers do not want their classes divided, nor do they want to change from a certain kind of lesson to the graded lessons. Not only do teachers and other workers sometimes interfere with grading, but the pupils can be a problem also. "I like my teacher and don't want to change," pouts one little girl. In one church where separate worship services for the children were being started, a boy in the Primary Department asked, "Why don't you old people like us any more? You won't let us meet with you."

You, as superintendent, must lead in solving these problems. The solution is to be sure that the board of Christian education, ministers, members of your staff, and faculty are consulted and "sold" on the plan of grading before any move is made. This selling can be done through personal conversation, workers' conferences, etc. Be sure the leaders unanimously agree on the grading plan. Then secure the approval of all the workers.

As you grade your Sunday school follow these basic rules:

1. Be sure that you understand what grading is and realize its importance.

2. "Sell" the board of Christian education and the minister on the importance of grading the school. They, like you, will have to know exactly what grading involves.

3. Develop the grading plan gradually. It is not a one-week, one-month, or even one-year project. It may take many years to grade the entire school so that it functions properly.

4. Hold a Promotion Day once each year to help you grade the school. On this day pupils are to be promoted from one class or department to another. Any Sunday in the year may be chosen. In the past most schools held Promotion Day on the last Sunday in September, just before Rally Day and the beginning of the first quarter of the graded lesson material. However, some schools are now holding Promotion Day on the last Sunday in June to correspond with the spring closing of public school. To help emphasize the principle of grading in your school make Promotion Day as elaborate as possible. Give some type of certificate and/or award to each pupil being promoted to impress him with the fact that he is making a step upward in spiritual progress.

As you grade your school and plan Promotion Day services remember that yours is a voluntary school. Pupils are not compelled by law to attend. You cannot force them to go from one class to another. You can only encourage them. You must show tolerance and make exceptions when you and members of your faculty are faced with the problem of a reluctant pupil. Surprisingly, the greatest problem will be with adult pupils. One of the most common questions asked at conferences of Sunday-school workers is this: "What can we do when there are grandparents in the young married couples' class?" One thing that can*not* be done is to promote the older pupils out of the class, unless the pupils have been trained over a long period of time to follow strict age limitations. Instead, start a class of younger pupils.

A necessary part of grading your school is appointing someone to be responsible for assigning each pupil to the proper class. When a new pupil visits for the first time he should be carefully interviewed and taken to a class. The pupil must not only understand why he is being sent to a certain class; he must be willing to go. A friendly secretary with an attractive personality can bring about such willingness in a new pupil.

Who is basically responsible for selecting the lesson materials or curriculum for the Sunday school? You can find out by reading this page.

What are Uniform Lessons? Read page 38.

Do you know what is meant by the term "group graded"? What other word can be used instead of "group"? The answers to these questions are on page 38.

What classes in the Sunday school are most likely to use elective courses? Why? Read the discussion of elective courses on pages 39 and 40.

How can you find out what lessons are best for your school? Page 41 contains information about how to select the best curriculum for the Sunday school.

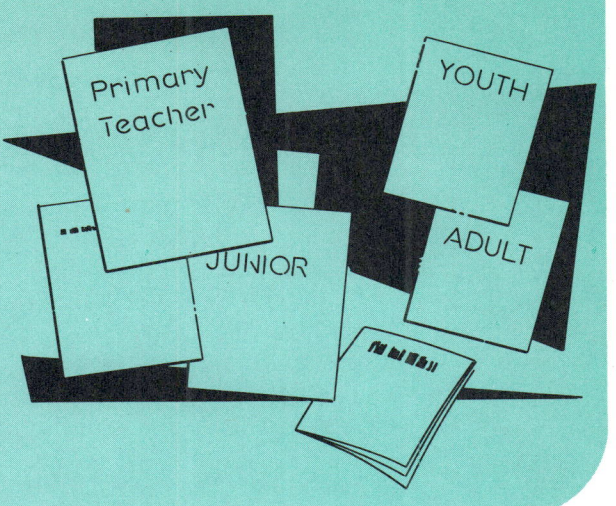

CHAPTER 4

YOU ORGANIZE

your school's teaching materials or curriculum

The Bible is the textbook of the Sunday school. But every teacher needs help in studying the Bible (theology), learning how to teach (pedagogy), and understanding the pupil (psychology). This help is provided by specially prepared lesson materials, or curriculum.

The selection of lesson materials rests in part with each teacher. The superintendent and minister also help to decide what materials are to be used. But the basic responsibility for selecting the curriculum belongs to the board of Christian education. Since this board acts as the overseer of the educational program, it must make the final decision regarding the nature and source of the lesson courses to be used. Even though departmental officers and teachers may be consulted about pictures, workbooks, flannelgraph materials, and other teaching helps, still the board is responsible for selecting the curriculum.

To help the board decide what kinds of lessons should be used in your school you need to become familiar with four kinds of courses commonly used in all Sunday schools. You also must learn about the advantages and disadvantages of each kind. These four kinds of lessons are as follows:

1. Uniform Lessons
2. Group-graded Lessons
3. Closely-graded Lessons
4. Elective Courses

Let us discuss each of these kinds of lessons for the Sunday school.

THE UNIFORM LESSONS

The word "uniform" explains the nature of these lessons. They offer a *uniform* subject for all classes above the Kindergarten. For instance, suppose the general theme of the Uniform Lessons for the quarter is "The Life of Christ." The lesson for the first Sunday could be "The Birth of Christ." This is the general, or overall theme. It must be taught, however, to different age groups. In other words, the lesson topic and treatment must be graded to apply to the grades or departments in your Sunday school.

For the Primary children the topic would be the simplest: "The Baby Jesus Is Born." The lesson story, pictures, and other teaching aids would be prepared especially for children in the Primary Department (first, second, and third-grade public school pupils).

For the Junior children the topic and treatment would be more advanced, perhaps with a topic such as "God's Gift to Us."

The Junior High topic and treatment would be fitted to the age: "What the Birth of Jesus Means to Me."

The High School or Senior Department might study "The Significance of Christ's Birth in the World Today."

For the older young people and adults the topic might be, "The Birth of Christ as the Fulfillment of Prophecy," with the lesson prepared accordingly.

The general lesson topic for the day is uniform throughout the Sunday school; but this topic is also graded in that it is prepared and taught to fit the particular ages and needs of each class. Actually, they are graded lessons with a uniform subject.

The Uniform Lessons are grouped together under certain themes that usually cover one or two quarters (three to six months). Over a six-year period the lessons provide a "through-the-Bible" course. Keep in mind that each lesson is closely connected with those preceding and following it. Remember also that in a school which uses the Uniform Lessons pupils may be promoted from one class to another without changing the general subject matter they have been studying.

GROUP-GRADED LESSONS

The key word here is "group." These lessons may also be referred to as departmentally graded. The lesson topics and the treatment of the lessons are graded to apply to an entire department or age group. For instance, a course is provided to meet the needs of the entire Nursery Department, another for the Kindergarten as a whole, etc.

In the strictly group-graded lessons different topics are chosen for each department; they are not uniform with those used in the other departments. As the pupil proceeds from one department to another using the group-graded lessons there is constant progression in his Christian development.

CLOSELY-GRADED LESSONS

The closely-graded lessons are different from all others in that they provide a different subject and lesson treatment for every Sunday of the pupil's life, from the time he is one year old until he is twenty-one or even older.

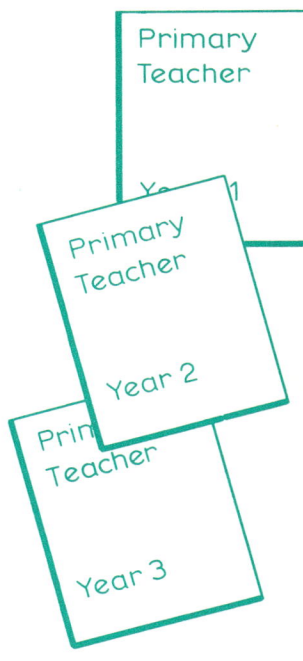

To illustrate: the pupils in the two age groups included in the Nursery Department do not have the same lesson topics and treatments as those found in the group-graded lessons. Instead, the two-year-olds have lessons prepared especially for children of that age. The three-year-olds, being one year older and a bit more advanced, study lessons prepared especially for them. The lesson topics and treatments are prepared to apply precisely to the age of the pupil. This progression is followed closely, year by year, until the pupil is a young adult. Remember the world "closely." The lessons are *closely* graded to fit the exact age of each pupil.

Closely-graded lessons can also be used in group-graded fashion in small schools. In a small school, for example, where there is only one class of boys and girls from six to eight years of age, the closely-graded Primary lessons could be used. The first year the class could study the first-year lessons in the closely-graded series. The next year the second-year lessons could be used, then the third-year lessons. A six-year old, coming into the Primary class when the third-year lessons are being taught would be studying lessons intended for an eight-year-old child (third grade). The eight-year olds, the next year, would be studying material prepared for six-year-olds (first grade). This is not an ideal arrangement; however, if the teacher is competent, it can be followed with success.

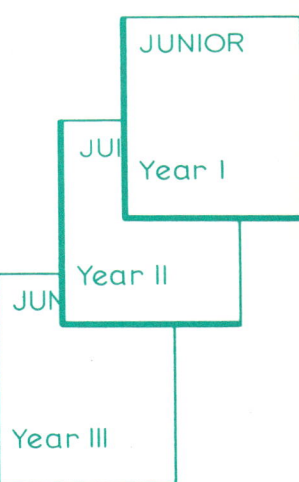

The closely-graded lesson year begins with the October quarter. Any class undertaking to study these lessons for the first time should do so on the first Sunday in October. Pupils promoted from one class to another studying the closely-graded lessons should be promoted to enter the new class when the graded year begins. These lessons offer a progressive study of Scripture without interruption, but this study is adapted to the various ages; therefore, each pupil is to move along so that he will always be studying the lessons prepared for his age group.

ELECTIVE COURSES

Elective courses are just what the name suggests. They are courses or topics that the students *elect* to study. They are unlike the others in that they are not published quarter-by-quarter and year-by-year.

Elective courses are chosen usually because of special interest in a certain subject, or for some timely purpose. A class of older young people or adults may become so interested in a discussion of church history that it wants to learn more. It can *elect* to abandon the regular Uniform Lessons for a period of time and study a book on church history. Many books on many subjects are available for worthwhile elective study in the Sunday school.

The use of an elective for some timely purpose is illustrated by the "Church Membership" class in the Sunday school. Those pupils aspiring to church membership, or church members who wish to increase their knowledge of the subject, may step out of their regular classes for a time and take this course. Classes in personal evangelism, Christian education in the home, stewardship, marriage relationships, parenthood, qualifications and duties of elders and deacons, and similar subjects aimed to achieve some special purpose, are becoming increasingly popular. Excellent courses are published for such purposeful studies.

Another type of Sunday-school lesson, used only in the rare case of a large class of men and/or women having a different teacher every Sunday, can be illustrated like this: One Sunday a temperance worker may deliver a lecture; the next, a judge in a domestic relations court; the next, an archaeologist, etc. Such a class is not a Sunday-school class in the accepted meaning of the term, but is the audience in a lecture series, or a public forum for the study and discussion of subjects that are unrelated except as they pertain to the general field of Christian education and influence.

To summarize, the four common types of lessons are the Uniform, the group-graded, and elective. The following chart illustrates the customary uses of each type of lesson.

☐ Commonly used ☐ Occasionally used
☐ Seldom used ☐ Not used at all

	Uniform Lessons	Group Graded	Closely Graded	Elective
CRADLE ROLL		Commonly used		
NURSERY		Occasionally used	Commonly used	
KINDERGARTEN		Occasionally used	Commonly used	
PRIMARY	Occasionally used	Seldom used	Commonly used	
JUNIOR	Occasionally used	Seldom used	Commonly used	
JUNIOR HIGH	Commonly used	Seldom used	Occasionally used	Seldom used
HIGH SCHOOL	Commonly used	Seldom used	Occasionally used	Occasionally used
YOUNG PEOPLE	Commonly used	Seldom used		Occasionally used
OLDER YOUNG PEOPLE	Commonly used	Seldom used		Occasionally used
ADULTS	Commonly used			Occasionally used

WHAT LESSONS ARE BEST FOR YOUR SCHOOL?

Your school probably uses more than one kind of lessons. The Cradle Roll and Nursery Departments may be using group-graded lessons; the Kindergarten, Primary, and Junior Departments may use closely-graded lessons; perhaps the Junior High and High School Departments are using the group-graded plan, while the older classes study from Uniform quarterlies. Some of the older classes may also study elective courses from time to time.

You and your faculty, working with the church's board of education, must decide which plan is best for each department or grade in your school. The chart on page 40 will help you. Following are some further suggestions:

The Uniform Lessons are most widely used, particularly in the classes of older pupils. Small churches with few classes and limited leadership prefer them. Because they are produced in such quantities, these lessons are quite inexpensive. In addition to the teachers' and pupils' quarterlies there are many visual aids available which can help in teaching the Uniform Lessons.

Educators prefer the closely-graded lessons because when they are used, each pupil is taught according to his stage of development. Also, each teacher specializes in one course, teaching it year after year. By doing this she and the school can accumulate a library of useful resource material for the lessons such as pictures, maps, flannelgraph materials, filmstrips, and slides.

The group or departmentally-graded lessons are reasonably well graded to each pupil's needs, and at the same time avoid some of the complex problems of close grading. They correspond with a department's worship programs, visual aids, observance of special days, and projects. For example, when a department uses the group-graded lessons the departmental superintendent can plan each worship service so that it will relate to the lesson topic for the day. When closely-graded lessons are used the superintendent cannot do this because each class studies a subject different from those studied in the other classes. Also, when group-graded lessons are used, the teachers in each department can share in planning and preparing their lessons.

The elective courses are used only when a group, usually a class of older pupils, decides to study a special subject. The time may come when all adult classes in the Sunday school will be studying a number of such courses and pupils will be able to attend the class that interests them most.

More details of these various kinds of lessons could be discussed, but it is not necessary. Your job is to acquaint your school with the best lessons available for the various departments, and to help select and use those best fitted to your needs.

Generally speaking, the younger classes will do their best work with the closely-graded and group-graded lessons, while the older young people and adults may prefer the Uniform and elective courses. As superintendent, you ought to consult the catalog of Sunday-school supplies, order samples of lesson literature, and study them. Then you can discuss the various kinds of lessons with your departmental leaders, helping them to select the best possible courses for their pupils.

Let us summarize this chapter with twelve suggestions regarding the literature used in your school:

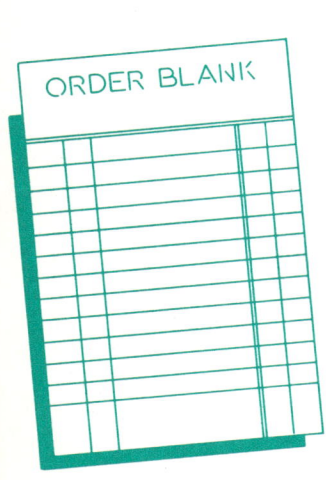

1. Carefully study the lesson situation in each department of your school. Learn what literature is being used. Then learn what other lessons are available. Discuss with the board of Christian education and the departmental leaders the lessons now being used and other available materials. Make sure that you and they understand all about the materials for each department.

2. Remember the purpose of your school. Counsel with your board of education to determine whether or not the literature used in your school is helping to achieve this purpose. There are many publishing houses and many approaches to the Bible. You and the board of education are responsible for seeing to it that the literature used in your school helps, rather than hinders, in the work of winning and conserving souls for Christ.

3. One person should order all the supplies for your Sunday school. This ordering must first be authorized. The order blanks supplied by the lesson publishers usually require that the name of the church be given, along with the name of the person who is to receive the literature, the one who orders the materials, and the one to whom the bill is to be sent. In order to avoid confusion, these names should not be changed unless it is really necessary.

4. Carefully review each order before it is sent. A good plan is for the purchasing agent to consult with each departmental head about the materials needed for the next quarter, then to confer with you regarding the order.

5. Check with the department heads to make sure that they and the teachers are taking full advantage of helps such as pictures, flannelgraph, filmstrips, slides, audio-visuals, superintendents' manuals, "take-home" papers, and parents' materials, in addition to the usual teachers' manuals and pupils' classbooks.

6. Watch the cost, but do not permit penny-pinching. Too long have Sunday schools been handicapped by false economy, hindering the Lord's work. A reasonable minimum to spend for each pupil is $2.50 per year, while $3.00 to $4.00 is better.

7. Be sure all lesson literature is ordered six weeks before it is to be used so the teachers can receive and study their materials at least two weeks before the new quarter begins.

8. Order adequately. There should be materials for all teachers, pupils, and departmental leaders, with an extra supply for new pupils and visitors. Do not be wasteful, but plan wisely.

9. See that each class or department has a cabinet or closet in which supplies can be kept neat and clean, ready for use. These supplies cost money—the Lord's money—and should receive the very best of care.

10. See to it that the lesson materials are used. Impress upon your faculty the fact that the church buys literature for a purpose, and that purpose is not accomplished unless the literature is put to the best possible use.

11. Supply your faculty with paper, pencils, Bibles, paste, chalk, crayons, chalkboards, maps, etc. The church or Sunday school is to pay for these materials. Teachers will usually do without these necessary teaching aids unless they are supplied by the church or school.

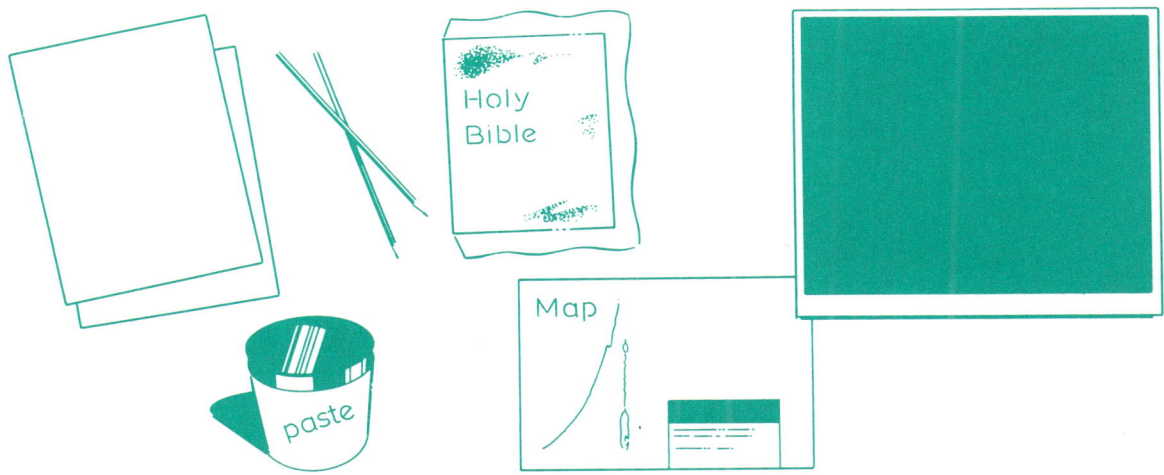

12. Have a plan for filing and keeping the teachers' manuals, pictures, etc., that can be used again. Money is often wasted on unnecessary purchases when this is not done.

You, as superintendent, are responsible for the school's accomplishing its purpose. The selection and use of lesson materials are important to the success of your school.

Remember this: There are more and better materials available for teaching the Bible than there are for teaching any other subject, whether it be mathematics, science, medicine, law, geography, or any other. The publishing houses have done a wonderful work in providing Sunday-school literature. Let us see that it is used to the glory of God.

How far in advance should a Sunday-school superintendent plan for the program of his school? After you read this page you should be able to answer this question.

How do you go about having your plans adopted? Page 45 contains information concerning presenting and adopting an annual program for the church and Sunday school.

Name some of the days which your school can observe in a special way. Most of these days come in the period between Easter and July. They are given on page 46.

What is "Stewardship Month"? Read page 47 to find out.

Can you give the four principles that apply to all types of Sunday morning programs? Read pages 49-51.

CHAPTER 5

YOU ORGANIZE

your school's program

"To fail to plan is to plan to fail," it has been said. This applies to the work of the Sunday school as well as to the business and professional world.

The city of Omaha once planned to level off the top of a hill on Dodge Street, so it notified the public utility companies that underground cables would have to be lowered to allow for a twenty-foot cut. The Northwestern Bell Telephone Company engineers replied that their company's cables were already at the proper depth. They had realized in advance what would have to be done some day, and had prepared for it. The engineers explained that their company made it a practice to plan ahead for twenty years.

As superintendent of the Sunday school you will not have to plan for the next twenty years, but you certainly should know what your school is to be doing for at least one whole year. You must know of the school's plans for each season and for each individual Sunday. You are responsible for your school's planning. Let us consider your plans for an entire year. Then we shall discuss how you should plan for each Sunday morning.

THE ANNUAL PROGRAM

As you plan your program for the coming year, you will want to consider the program of the entire church. As we have said, your school is a part of the church—an important part. The success of the church's plans for the year depends largely upon the co-operation of the Sunday school. It is your job to encourage your staff of workers to give this co-operation.

YOU ORGANIZE

The minister usually outlines an entire year's program for the church. He presents it to the board of officers for discussion and adoption. You should be present for the discussion, or at least talk with the minister and perhaps the chairman of the board of officers about your school's part in the plans. Introduce the proposed plans to the board of Christian education and to your faculty. After they have discussed them with you, return them, along with your suggestions and recommendations, to the minister. Before the annual program is finally adopted it should be submitted for suggestions to as many different workers and groups as possible. These suggestions are then considered by the minister and perhaps a committee composed of you and other leading workers. When the program has been revised (if it needs revising), the minister will submit it again to the board of officers who will in turn recommend the revised program to the entire congregation for adoption.

Perhaps you are wondering why all this action is necessary. First, the church wants a plan that is workable. To form such a plan, as many leaders and workers as possible ought to be consulted. Second, if the plan is to succeed, it must have unanimous approval from all workers so that there will be a maximum of co-operation. If they are included in the planning they will feel more responsibility for making the plan succeed.

Such planning takes time, especially when there has been no annual program in the past. Once a plan is adopted, however, it can be reconsidered each year, changed in certain places, and used again. Following is a year's program used by a congregation that realizes the importance of the Sunday school:

January—Easter: During this period an annual ten-week campaign or crusade was conducted, during which every member of the congregation was contacted each week by means of a letter, the telephone, or a personal visit. These contacts were made by a team of "captains." Each captain received a card bearing five names, with the address and telephone number of each person named. Every week it was each captain's responsibility to contact the five people named on his card. Every two weeks the captains exchanged cards so that each captain came into contact twice with each church member. Even the captains' names were on the cards. An attendance record was kept, and each week the list of captains was published in the church paper, along with the attendance record of each group. The captain whose groups achieved the best record was commended publicly.

The entire church program was centered around this campaign. The minister preached a special series of sermons during the ten weeks; public and private prayers were offered for the success of the campaign; the Sunday school, Sunday evening groups, etc., worked hard to make the campaign successful; teachers and officers in the Sunday school kept it constantly before their classes. The campaign was given a different title each year, such as "Ten Weeks with Christ," or "Victory Through Loyalty." Usually the campaign was brought to a close with a week or two of evangelistic services held each evening just preceding Easter Sunday.

These activities during the ten weeks greatly stimulated interest and attendance in the Sunday school. Attendance goals for each class were set for each Sunday and the pupils were challenged to achieve the goals. As the campaign progressed the goals were set higher and higher.

Easter—July: Special days were given prominence during this period. Easter Sunday, always a day of high attendance in most churches, was followed by a "Better than Easter Sunday," when an effort was made to avoid a slump by trying to surpass the Easter attendance. Thus a program of growing achievement was maintained.

Attendance goals were also set for special days such as Mother's Day, Children's Day, Father's Day, and Patriotic Sunday (the Sunday immediately preceding the Fourth of July). There was no let-down in the activity of the school. Its high attendance carried over into the worship services and helped to stimulate all the work of the church.

During the spring season the church made special appeals to individuals to commit themselves to Christ. To help with these appeals the Sunday school offered a class in church membership for prospective members. Of course anyone was permitted to attend. The school also helped by giving the minister and evangelistic workers a list of all pupils who were not members of the church, along with the names and addresses of those in their families who might be prospects. Teachers of older pupils stressed the evangelistic appeal in their lessons; classes gave their pupils prayer lists containing names of people who were not Christians. All of the work done by the school was directed by the superintendent, in close co-operation with the minister. Sunday-school pupils were won for Christ.

In June the Sunday school played an important part in making the vacation Bible school a success. It provided most of the teachers and many of the pupils.

July and August: These are the months of the dreaded "summer slump" in Sunday-school attendance. To avoid an attendance slump the Sunday school set a goal to maintain an attendance level at least fifteen percent above the school's average for July and August of the preceding year. Each class was given a certain goal to reach on every Sunday of the two months.

To dramatize its effort, the school entered a nation-wide anti-summer-slump contest sponsored by the weekly Sunday-school paper that was distributed by the school every Sunday. In doing this, the school not only competed with its own record for the previous year, but with other schools of its size throughout the nation.

Because summer is such a difficult season for the Sunday school the superintendent recognized the necessity for extra effort on the part of all workers. He planned to promote attendance by using the mails, the telephone, and a program of personal calling. He conducted a class to help the teachers improve their teaching methods.

September: This was called "Homecoming Month." A special effort was made to have every regularly enrolled member of the school present every Sunday. The month's activities led up to Promotion Day on the last Sunday in the month, and to the annual Rally Day, on the first Sunday in October. If the church planned a "Homecoming Day" program the Sunday school did its part by contacting former members who had moved out of the city, asking them to send greetings.

October: This was called "Rally Month." The church held a two-week evangelistic meeting beginning on Rally Day. The Sunday school urged all pupils to attend the meeting regularly. On the final Sunday of the meeting an effort was made to achieve a record-breaking attendance in the school. Under the superintendent's leadership the school endeavored to enroll as many new pupils as possible during October, as well as to maintain a high percentage of regular attendance on the part of the enrolled members.

During October, also, the Sunday school observed an annual "Teacher Appreciation Week." Every teacher and officer of the school received special recognition at a special program.

November: This was known as "Stewardship Month." It led up to the annual solicitation of pledges to support the financial program of the church during the coming year. "Stewardship Day" was observed on the Sunday before Thanksgiving. During Thanksgiving week pledges were solicited. The Sunday-school superintendent urged every officer and teacher to make a pledge to give regularly to the Lord's work. Then in turn he urged the pupils to do the same, explaining how the money was to be used, how much was needed, and why they should all participate.

December: As you would expect, the Sunday school was busy making plans and preparations for Christmas. But it was not too busy to take an active part in the annual "Consecration Month." Each December the church and Sunday school urged every member and pupil to dedicate himself to the success of the coming year's program. The Sunday school explained the program to all its pupils from the Juniors to the oldest adults, and showed each one how he could help make it succeed. All pupils, teachers, officers, and other workers were asked to pray regularly for the success of the work ahead and to give their own time and talents to it.

At Christmas the Sunday-school pupils brought food, money, and clothing to be distributed to poor people in the congregation and in the community. The superintendent's benevolence committee handled all the arrangements. Another committee, made up of young people, provided a "post office" for Christmas greeting cards exchanged among church and Sunday-school members. Those who used this convenience (and there were many) were asked to give to the youth fund the amount of money they would ordinarily have spent on postage stamps. The fund was used for social activities of the young people, to pay expenses to Christian service camps, to help students in Bible colleges, to help buy equipment for the youth department, and in many other worthwhile ways.

The Sunday school sponsored a special Christmas program consisting of recitations, songs, and playlets by the children and young people. The year was brought to a close with a watch-night prayer meeting and social hour for the entire church and Sunday school.

Reviewing this plan we find that a Sunday school's annual program can be planned to include any or all of these special events:

January—Easter: Loyalty campaign to encourage regular attendance by every church member.

Easter—July: Enlistment of new pupils; special days observed.

July and August: Summer attendance campaign with a goal to maintain an average attendance of at least fifteen percent above the average for the same two months of the previous year.

September: "Homecoming Month," in which the Sunday school strives to have every member of the school in attendance every Sunday. The month's program ends with Promotion Day.

October: Emphasis on recruiting new members to both the church and Sunday school. This is a good time to hold an installation and appreciation service for teachers and officers and to start new classes.

November: "Stewardship Month," in which the Sunday school urges its leaders and pupils to support the church's financial program for the coming year.

December: "Consecration Month," for the purpose of urging all pupils to dedicate themselves to making the program for the coming year a success.

An annual program may be launched at any time. The graded year begins with October in most schools, and is therefore chosen by some as the best time to launch the annual program. Others follow the calendar year, and still others hold Promotion Day in June and begin the new school year with the first Sunday in July.

Heed these words of caution: Do not "bite off more than you can chew." That is, do not undertake too much. It is better to succeed with a program of few projects than to fail with a program of many. Also—and this is worth repeating—ask as many leading workers as possible to participate in outlining the program. Then keep the coming objectives constantly before them so that they can plan ahead.

The year's program should center around the church's objective: to recruit and conserve Christians. Of course the Sunday school cannot very well help to achieve this goal if there are few new people attending its classes. This is why there is so much emphasis placed on attendance. The annual program should also include such important activities as training leaders, improving equipment, dividing classes, rearranging departments, and financing the school. These are vital steps in the progress of your school and require very careful planning.

To keep your year's program moving, work out a time schedule by which the various plans and projects are to be completed. You will have to set up a system for filing notations and records, and for reminding yourself of the activities coming up.

YOU ORGANIZE

THE SUNDAY MORNING PROGRAM

The annual program is outlined once a year. Each month the school's teachers and officers meet to review the program, make necessary adjustments, and plan specific activities. Every week, however, you, the superintendent, face the problem of the program for the coming Sunday morning.

There are almost as many kinds of Sunday-morning programs as there are Sunday schools. Some schools hold the traditional opening assembly, followed by the class sessions and a brief closing service. In others, each department holds its own opening and closing sessions as well as the teaching period. Many churches provide both departmental worship services and teaching sessions on Sunday morning.

Certain principles apply to all types of programs. These can be summed up in four words: Purpose, planning, promptness, and participation.

First let us consider four *purposes* of the Sunday morning program: inspiration, training, education, and publicity. Since we have talked about the purpose of the lesson period, we shall discuss these purposes in connection with the opening session.

INSPIRATION. (You may prefer the term "worship.") Before an important football game a high school or college holds an assembly period or pep session at which the students unite in their determination to win. Their sense of union and common interest is an inspiration as they strive to achieve a definite goal. A Sunday school is made up of people with a common objective. These people can be inspired or encouraged to reach their objective by singing together, praying together, etc., in the opening service. The element of worship enters into these activities, but is incidental when we remember that the Sunday school is the church at study, and that the church gathers for another Sunday morning service for worship.

The inspirational part of the opening service usually consists of the following things:

1. Hymns. These should be carefully selected in advance to carry out the educational theme of the day. They should be led by an experienced song leader who will not be afraid to introduce new hymns.

2. Prayer. Select and notify in advance a suitable person to lead in a brief prayer. You may wish to tell him the theme for the service so that he can word his prayer accordingly. Urge each person who leads in prayer to keep the work and needs of the Sunday school in mind. Strive for variety in the prayer program. The habitual use of one prayer or one person will make the services dull and monotonous. Sentence prayers, prayer hymns and responses, prayers quoted from the Bible are some of the many variations that can be used.

3. Scripture Reading. One person may read a brief passage of Scripture that fits the theme; or the leader and audience can read responsively. Perhaps occasionally a class can give a choral reading or recitation of an appropriate passage of Scripture.

4. <u>Special Feature</u>. It is not always necessary to have a special feature, but is recommended if it can tie in with the theme of the day. Vocal numbers, readings, and recitations can be used.

5. <u>Announcements</u>. The most important thing to remember about making announcements is that they can be brief and to the point. Give the audience an opportunity to add to the announcements or to ask for more information concerning those that have been given. Every superintendent ought to study and learn the art of making announcements so they will be enjoyed and remembered. The booklet, *How to Make Announcements*, will help you. Limit the announcements to things that concern the entire Sunday school. Avoid monotony by asking others to make the announcements occasionally.

Remember to vary the order of procedure often to stimulate interest, discourage tardiness, and give each service an identity of its own.

TRAINING. Perhaps you have not realized it before, but the opening service is an important training school. Many church pianists and organists, soloists, choir members, began using their talents in this brief period. Perhaps you learned how to preside when you were an assistant superintendent. Many people who are especially adept at praying in public learned to do so in the opening Sunday school service. As you plan each Sunday's program select the personnel with their development in mind as well as their immediate effectiveness.

EDUCATION. Every song, prayer, and announcement should contribute to the teaching aim of the day. Even if many classes that will be studying many different lesson topics are involved, one central thought can be used to emphasize all these topics. The opening period is a teaching period just as the class period is. To use the period to the best educational advantage, much prayer on your part and careful planning either by you or a responsible committee are required.

PUBLICITY. There must be some time given to promote the cause of the school or department. The opening assembly period is the time. Goals for the day may be emphasized along with the announcements of goals for the coming week or month. Of course, all meetings pertaining to the school or department should be announced. Visitors may be introduced and recognition given for outstanding achievement.

Now let us consider the *planning* that is so necessary for a successful Sunday morning program. Needless to say, if you do not plan thoroughly and properly, chaos, or at the least, monotony, will result. Before the opening of the Sunday morning program in one church the minister said to me, "I can tell you within ten words what the superintendent will say this morning." He told me. I listened. Sure enough, he had quoted the superintendent almost word for word. That superintendent had not planned his program. As a result, terrible monotony pervaded the entire school.

The Sunday morning program includes the opening, study period, reports, and closing. All these take place within one hour. Whether yours is a small or large school, these four parts are necessary, and you are responsible for their success. A public school principal supervises many grades and classes. Each class meets separately with its own teacher, but the principal is responsible for their success. The Sunday-school superintendent has a similar responsibility.

Besides the careful plans that you have been making all week, you must prepare in the following ways to insure the success of the Sunday morning program:

1. Check every classroom to make sure everything is ready for the classes.
2. Be sure all staff members and teachers are to be present. If some are not, secure suitable substitutes.
3. Appoint "greeters" to welcome all pupils and see that they are ushered to the proper places.
4. Meet with your faculty for a pre-session prayer period.

The third principle for a successful Sunday morning program—*promptness*—is often overlooked. But the necessity to begin and close the school on time cannot be stressed too much. Even if the pianist, song leader, or janitor are not there, BEGIN ON TIME. Let everyone understand that the school begins exactly when it is supposed to begin and closes exactly when it is supposed to close. Beginning on time will discourage tardiness; closing promptly will contribute to the success of the church's other Sunday morning activities. The Sunday-school hour can be divided like this:

Opening period—five to fifteen minutes.

Study period—thirty to fifty minutes.

Reports—these are either posted on the bulletin board, announced by the minister in the worship hour, or included with the closing period, so the time need not be counted.

Closing—Five to fifteen minutes. If the worship hour follows the Sunday school period each class can hold its own closing. If the Sunday school follows the worship hour the classes may or may not wish to gather together for a closing session.

From the public schools we have inherited the buzzer, or bell system, of signals. These signals are used by the superintendent or someone he appoints, to warn teachers and classes that the lesson period is ending. Sometimes a signal sounds a few minutes before the closing to allow time for the teacher to finish the lesson, make announcements, and bring the session to an orderly close. Whether a warning signal should be used, and if so, how far in advance of the closing, is for the superintendent and his faculty to decide.

The final principle—*participation*—is important also. Be sure that as many people as possible take part in the Sunday morning program. This applies to pupils as well as teachers and other workers. If each person feels that he is actually taking part in the program of the school he will be more interested in its success.

Let us summarize by saying that the secret to a successful program, whether it be annual or weekly, is to plan *in advance*. The superintendent who carefully and prayerfully plans in advance, includes his fellow workers in the planning, and gives detailed attention to carrying out the plans, will succeed.

Section 3

you deputize

Chapter 6—Helpers
　　Where Are Workers to Be Found?
　　How Can Workers Be Discovered?

Chapter 7—Officers
　　Qualifications of Officers
　　Selection of Officers
　　Term of Office
　　Duties of Officers

Chapter 8—Teachers
　　Selecting Teachers
　　Qualifications of Teachers
　　Duties of Teachers
　　Your Responsibilities Toward Your Teachers

Chapter 9—By Training Officers and Teachers
　　How to Train Christians to be Officers and Teachers

Chapter 10—By Rewarding Officers and Teachers
　　Installation Service
　　Appreciation Service

What is the chief cause of failure among Sunday-school superintendents? Read the first paragraph below.

Why should a Sunday-school superintendent enlist helpers? Four reasons are listed on this page.

Do you realize how many duties the superintendent of a Sunday school has? On page 55 you can read some of the many things he must do, or be responsible for, during the week and every Sunday morning.

Into what two general categories are Sunday-school workers placed? You can find out by reading page 56.

Name some of the plans and suggestions for discovering workers and helpers for the Sunday school. These plans are given for you on pages 57 and 58.

CHAPTER 6

YOU DEPUTIZE

helpers

What would you say is the chief cause of failure among Sunday-school superintendents? Is it lack of consecration? No. Then is it laziness? No. *It is the failure to let others take responsibility, and failure to supervise those who are given responsibility.* The superintendent fails when he tries to be "Mr. Do-it-all." Unable to do it, he becomes discouraged and quits.

If you are a wise superintendent, you will never do anything that you can enlist someone else to do. There are several good reasons for this:

1. *To save yourself.* After all, you are only one person, and have only twenty-four hours in each day. Don't try to do everything.

2. *To save your school.* Many Sunday schools suffer because the superintendent tries to do everything. He "spreads himself too thin."

3. *To save your fellow workers.* "Use me or lose me" is as true in Sunday school as it is anywhere else. The growing Christian is the working Christian. Part of your job is to put everyone to work.

4. *To boost attendance.* In the Sunday school there is what is known as "the rule of ten." That is, a quick check in almost any school will show that the attendance is approximately ten times the number of teachers and other workers. This means that the more workers you engage the larger the attendance will be.

No factory superintendent would try to run every machine in the factory. No band leader would try to play every instrument in the band at once. The measure of a good superintendent, a good band leader, or a good manager in any job is his ability to discover, choose, and train a staff of helpers. Henry Ford, who revolutionized the automobile industry in its early days, was said to have succeeded because he knew how to discover, choose, and train men to head up the various activities and departments of a multi-billion-dollar enterprise. The same praise can be given to most successful business men. They know how to deputize others to help them fulfill their many responsibilities.

In one small church that wished to improve its Sunday school I found the minister acting as superintendent. He arrived early every Sunday morning, opened the doors, lit the fires, distributed the hymnbooks, turned on the lights in the classrooms, greeted the arrivals, led the singing, made the announcements, offered the prayer, and complained that "no one in the church is able to do these things, so I have to do them." It was easy to tell that minister and his Sunday school that the first step toward improvement was to deputize helpers.

Your job as superintendent has many detailed responsibilities. They range from housekeeping to song-leading; from planning to bookkeeping; from presiding to publicizing; from financing to ushering. The job as superintendent requires willingness to work, ability to lead, patience with people, planning with purpose, and prayerful contact with God. It is not an easy task, but it is worthwhile. It is a seven-days-a-week, twenty-four-hours-a-day job.

During the week you must attend general workers' conferences and departmental conferences, check records, see what progress is being made in the programs underway, call in the homes of workers and perhaps some pupils, confer with the minister and the board of Christian education, prepare for the coming Sunday's program, read articles and books pertaining to the Sunday school, attend workshops, clinics, conferences, and conventions several times a year, and take care of a multitude of details.

On Sunday morning you must make sure that the classrooms are clean and ready for use, all arrivals are welcomed properly, a record is made of visitors and new pupils, the places of absent teachers and officers are properly filled, and that everything is ready before the school begins. Then comes the opening assembly with its program of music, devotions, announcements, special feature, and the class sessions with attention to order and discipline. Maintaining records of attendance, studying the records, receiving, recording, and accounting for the offering, seeing that supplies are ordered, delivered on time, and properly distributed and used, are a few of the many detailed responsibilities belonging to the superintendent.

This is by no means a complete list of the superintendent's duties, but it is complete enough to show that he needs helpers. The number of helpers and their duties will vary, depending upon the size of the school and the number of workers available. In a small school with few workers, the number of workers will be small and each will have several responsibilities. In a larger school there will be more workers, each having fewer responsibilities. In every school, however, regardless of size, the work is the same. Every school must have teachers. Every school requires secretarial work. Every school needs a treasurer. Every school has to purchase and maintain equipment. Every school requires literature, and therefore, a librarian.

POTENTIAL SUNDAY-SCHOOL WORKERS

The superintendent of every school, large or small, needs helpers. These helpers must have the same qualifications and perform the same tasks regardless of the size of the school. The only difference is that one worker in a small school will perform several duties, while a worker in a large school may have only one duty.

The superintendent's helpers may be listed in two categories:

Officers. These are workers who either do not teach, or if they do teach, have additional responsibility. They are the office force, supervisors, and foremen of the factory that is the Sunday school.

Included in the group of officers are the assistant superintendent, song leaders and musicians, secretary, treasurer, librarian, ushers, departmental superintendents, activity chairmen, and all others who look directly to the general superintendent for leadership.

Teachers. These workers look to their departmental superintendents for supervision. Of course, in a small school where the teachers are also departmental superintendents, the general superintendent will probably have direct contact with the teachers. Otherwise, he deals directly with the departmental superintendents and only indirectly with the teachers. But even though the superintendent does not deal directly with the teachers, he is still responsible for them as well as all the other workers in the Sunday school.

Where are these workers to be found? They are all around us. One of the tragedies in most churches is the failure to make use of potential manpower. In even the smallest congregation there is power to inspire the whole town, city, or county if each member would just measure up to his capabilities as a Christian. A man in a big church near Chicago had the training and background to teach, but there was no place for him on the Sunday-school faculty. With the encouragement of the minister and board of officers he set up a Sunday afternoon Bible class in a nearby community where there was a rapidly growing population. Soon his class of adults included children. He called upon his home church to send helpers to conduct a Sunday school. Among the helpers who were selected was a young man, unnoticed before this, who was to be superintendent of the new Sunday school. This young man was a door-to-door salesman for a popular brush company. He immediately put into practice in the Sunday school those things he had learned in his work. The Sunday school began at once to grow and soon there was a new church established. It is interesting to note that the young salesman's experience as superintendent of the new Sunday school so increased his ability that he was promoted to be district manager for his company.

Said the man who was telling about the growth of the new church, "We found our workers in the older and larger church. They were people who were just drifting along doing nothing. But when they were given a chance, they proved to be wonderful workers for the Lord." Wasted manpower is a tragedy existing in almost every church.

How can workers be discovered? Several plans are suggested. One is an annual service enlistment campaign. Every Christian ought to be a worker for the Lord. The purpose of the campaign is to enlist everyone in the church to do the job in which he is most interested and for which he is best fitted. To carry out such a campaign, a "Volunteer Service Enlistment Blank" is prepared. It contains a list of church activities under such headings as "General Church Administration," "Christian Education," "Group Leadership," and "General Services."

Under "Christian Education" are listed teaching the various age groups, secretarial work, song leading, promotion or publicity, and missionary, social, and recreational activities.

Every member of the church is asked to study the enlistment blank, and to check the fields of service "in which I will continue to serve," or "for which I will prepare to serve as called upon." Before the lists are distributed the minister may introduce the campaign by preaching a sermon on a subject such as "Be Worthy of Your Vocation," using Ephesians 4:1 as a text.

One busy church provided a service enlistment blank for every new member. He was asked to indicate which activity he preferred. He was then put into a training class to prepare for that activity. Or, if he was already qualified, he was immediately put to work. This church strove to make the following statement a reality: "Every member has a job for which he alone is responsible."

In another church the superintendent, minister, and board of Christian education adopted this plan:

1. Once a year they went through the entire church roll and composed a list of potential staff members and teachers.

2. A training program was established for all present and potential workers.

3. Pupils in every class of the Sunday school were taught and encouraged to participate in their lesson periods, and thus were helped to develop the desire and ability to serve.

4. Assistant helpers were enlisted in all departments and activities to be trained for the positions of teachers and officers.

5. Associate officers and teachers were given the opportunity every few weeks to serve as the regular officers and teachers.

6. Vacation Bible school employed as many helpers as possible. Many of these developed into Sunday-school workers.

7. Young people who had attended summer Christian service camps were given something special to do in the Sunday school.

8. These three facts were used to induce people to serve:
   a. Every Christian ought to be a worker for the Lord.
   b. There is a great need for workers, and we owe obedience to the Lord who has done so much for us.
   c. A definite stewardship of talent is required of us.

Once the workers were enlisted, the joy of serving helped to keep them faithful in their tasks and responsibilities.

9. Appointments were made for one-year periods so that the officers and teachers could be changed if they so desired or if the superintendent and board of Christian education thought it advisable.

Of course there are many other methods for enlisting workers for the Sunday school. Your job is to help develop the one that is best for your church. Whatever method you select, be sure to impress upon the mind of each worker the importance of the responsibility he is about to accept. He must realize the necessity for his fulfilling his responsibility properly. As you make your selection of helpers keep these suggestions in mind:

1. *Look before you leap*. Be careful. It is easy to give responsibility to the wrong person, but it is difficult to remove an incompetent worker. Know the person and evaluate his experience and ability before making a specific assignment.

2. *Be sure the prospective helper is a team-worker*. An analysis of four-thousand discharged workers in industry showed that only about one-third of them lost their jobs because they lacked ability. The other two-thirds were dismissed because they did not get along with their fellow workers.

3. *Don't be a cradle snatcher*. Too often we are tempted to place young people in responsible positions before they are ready, simply because they seem to be willing. Be sure every prospective helper is qualified before giving him a job in the Sunday school.

4. *Employ both men and women*. It is true that men can do some types of church work better than women. But in the Sunday school women are as capable as men to teach and perform the other necessary tasks. However, do not overload your staff with women. Put the men to work too.

5. *Beware of the novice*. A newcomer into the ranks, no matter how promising, must not be enlisted and put to work too quickly. He may have weaknesses that are not apparent at first, and he may cause older members and workers to be offended.

6. *Try to use each prospective worker as an assistant in a position* before burdening him with the full responsibility of an important job.

7. *Arrange for a new worker to be carefully coached in the work he is to do*. Lack of such coaching can result in a feeling of incompetency and frustration, leading to discouragement and failure.

8. *Pray to God about each prospective worker*. If you will keep in close contact with the Lord He will help you as you select your workers for the Sunday school.

9. *Discuss each proposed appointment with others*, such as the minister, members of the board of education, departmental workers, and staff members who will be closely associated with the new worker.

10. *Be loyal to your deputies*. Back them up. Encourage them when they are discouraged. Praise them at every opportunity. Stand up for them when they are criticized. Loyalty to your helpers will encourage teamwork and will help to accomplish the great task before you.

Into what two general groups can officers of the Sunday school be divided? The second paragraph of this page names and describes these two groups.

What are the qualifications of a Sunday-school officer? Why is each qualification important? Read page 60 for the answers to these questions.

How should Sunday-school officers be selected; how long should the term of office be? Read pages 60 and 61.

Can you name the duties of the assistant superintendent? Page 61 gives them for you.

Name some of the duties of the "literature librarian." They may be found on page 63.

What three types of records must be kept by the secretarial and bookkeeping staff? See page 64 for the answer.

CHAPTER 7

YOU DEPUTIZE

officers

Every Sunday school has officers and teachers. If a school is very small, an officer may also be a teacher.

The officers can be divided into two general groups. One group is described as *organizational*; the other is *functional*. The organizational officers are those who are at the heads of the school's various departments and are known as departmental superintendents. The functional officers are those who have specific duties to perform. Included in this group are the assistant superintendent, secretary, treasurer, librarian, song leader, pianist, and the chairmen of such committees as missions, benevolent, and recreation.

The officers report directly to the superintendent and are under his personal supervision. They are to him what the cabinet of the United States is to the president. They are the superintendent's cabinet. In large, well-organized schools they sometimes meet as a cabinet, apart from the general staff meetings which the teachers also attend. Some schools hold weekly cabinet meetings in addition to the monthly workers' conferences.

Generally speaking, all Sunday schools have the same type of work to be done. Therefore, they need the same types of officers. In a small school, however, one person may hold two or more offices. For instance, the school's secretary may also be the treasurer and librarian. In a large school each officer will probably have only one basic responsibility. For example, one person will be the secretary, another the treasurer, still another the librarian, etc. The various officers and their duties will be discussed later in this chapter.

QUALIFICATIONS OF OFFICERS

In addition to having experience, training, and a vital interest in the work to be done, an officer in the Sunday school must meet the following requirements:

1. *Be a Christian*. An officer is a leader. He is also looked up to. For that reason he must be a worthy example to others. Also, he is not paid for his work as the world measures payment. He serves because he loves the Lord, desires to do the Lord's will, is concerned about the souls of others, and wants to recruit people to Christ and help them remain faithful. Only a Christian can have these motives for serving.

2. *Be a member of the local church*. In a small church where leadership is a problem, or in a large church where professional ability is the chief requirement, this qualification of membership in the local church may be objected to an non-essential. Yet, considering the question from a practical angle, how can a salesman sell a product which he personally declines to use? Not only is the officer to be a member of the local congregation, he is to be an *active, supporting* member, who participates in the entire program of the church, giving of his time, talent, and possessions in such a way as to leave no doubt regarding his affiliations.

3. *Be a team worker*. Every athletic team has a captain or manager who calls the signals or tells the players what to do. Each player in turn does his part to help win the game. On the Sunday-school team the superintendent calls the signals. Each officer is to do his part to make the team successful. He may do his work in his own way if he wants to—and he will probably do better work if he is encouraged to use his initiative. But he must work as a member of the team. Some people seem to be trouble makers by nature. They are always rebelling, complaining, and finding fault. Such people are poor officer material.

4. *Be dependable*. Tardiness, frequent and unannounced absences, and failure to carry out assignments are fatal to a person's being a successful and competent officer in the Sunday school. Be sure that a prospective officer is dependable before assigning him to an important job.

5. *Be willing to improve*. No officer is ever perfect. Every officer ought to be eager and willing to study and work for improvement in carrying out his responsibilities.

SELECTION OF OFFICERS

The superintendent is to be elected by the congregation, or at least selected by the congregation's board of Christian education. The other officers of the Sunday school may be appointed by the board of Christian education or recommended by that board for election at a workers' conference. Either way, the superintendent must have a definite part in the selection, since each officer is to be under his supervision. These officers are the superintendent's "right-hand men." He ought to insist upon having a part in their selection.

TERM OF OFFICE

Each officer, including the superintendent, is elected for one year. His term ends with the close of the Sunday-school year, when he may or may not be selected for another year.

The length of his service in a particular office depends on his fitness. As long as he is the best person available for the position, he ought to keep it. When there is another who can do the work better, then he should give it up.

Many problems can arise when one person is required to give his office to another. Some people assume that certain positions are theirs by inheritance, or tradition, or habit; and they personally resent being replaced. Such an attitude can be avoided if all officers go out of office at the end of the year and must be elected again before being returned to office. After several years, if changes are made frequently, the problem will no doubt be lessened but may not be entirely eliminated. Sometimes the less competent person can be assigned to another position so that one with more ability can take his place. Another solution is to appoint a promising prospect as assistant to a certain office so that the regular office holder will either improve or let the assistant take over.

DUTIES OF OFFICERS

The various officers of the Sunday school are listed on this and the following pages along with the duties they must perform.

Assistant Superintendent. There may be one or more assistant superintendents, depending upon the size of the school and the number and kind of duties involved. An assistant superintendent's main task is to learn the job of regular superintendent so that he can some day qualify for that job. He must understand and participate in all of the regular superintendent's activities, sitting in on meetings with the board of education, helping plan the school's program, and perhaps assisting in the selection and training of other staff members.

In some schools there is an assistant superintendent who directs the Sunday-morning program, another who is in charge of attendance, and still another who works with the departments and teachers, and is responsible for classrooms and equipment. Many superintendents have their assistants preside on Sunday morning, leaving them free to observe the work of the entire school. Sometimes there is an assistant who supervises the expanded or extended program of the Sunday school.

The important thing is that the assistant superintendent be given specific and important responsibilities. The general superintendent's job is to help the assistant serve with success.

Departmental Superintendents and Members of Their Staffs. As general superintendent, you will find these departmental superintendents of the utmost help. You may not know what makes a Junior behave as he does, but the Junior Department's superintendent knows. Perhaps

you do not know how the teen-agers can help make your school's program succeed, but the leaders of these interesting boys and girls can tell you and can direct them in doing their part. As general superintendent, you probably will read books on Christian education that will give you a limited understanding of each age group. For detailed leadership of the age groups, however, you depend on your departmental superintendents.

Just as you are responsible for the school as a whole, each departmental head is responsible for his entire department. You are not to by-pass them, or "go over their heads," but you are to work with them. You are to deal with the teachers, pupils, and departmental officers through the departmental superintendents.

Just as you have your general staff for the entire school, the departmental superintendents have their staffs, including musicians, secretaries, etc. For obvious reasons, the departmental leaders are to have a voice in the selection of their staffs. They are not to make the selections alone, but with your approval and that of the board of Christian education.

Again, the superintendent of the small school may be saying, "This is well and good for the large school, but ours is a small school." Even the smallest school has departments. These departments, even in a school having only thirty in atttendance, must have superintendents. Each superintendent may be the only teacher in his department. He may also do all the secretarial and other work in the department. But the work is there to be done, just as in a large school. The general superintendent will deputize departmental responsibility in a small school as in a large school. He cannot do all the work by himself. He therefore must have these departmental deputies to help him.

Song Leader, Musicians, Program Committee. A pianist, song leader, and a person or committee to plan the opening assembly programs are essential officers in the Sunday school. Whether the school meets by departments or together in one assembly, these same people are needed. In the school's assembly the general superintendent is responsible for selecting the musicians and program committee. In the departmental assemblies, each departmental superintendent has this responsibility.

The duties of the song leader and musicians need little discussion. The song leader must be able to select appropriate hymns for each Sunday's theme, teach new hymns, and direct the hymns in such a way that the audience will want to sing their best. The musicians (pianist or organist) of course accompany the singing of hymns and prepare the people for the services with appropriate preludes.

The duties of the person or committee that plans the opening assembly program are these:

1. To decide on contents and theme of the program.

2. To select and ask appropriate persons to lead in prayer, read Scripture, present the special feature, make announcements, etc.

3. To make sure the theme of the day is carried out in each part of the program.

The general superintendent can, of course, plan the Sunday-morning assembly programs. But it is better if he appoints another person or group of people to plan the services. Perhaps the song leader and pianist can work with the superintendent as a program committee.

Librarian. Two kinds of library work are found in the Sunday school. One is the responsibility for ordering and distributing the quarterly, monthly, and weekly literature. The other is taking care of library books, projectors, film strips, slides, flannelgraph materials, and supplies of paper, paste, scissors, chalk, etc.

The responsibility for ordering and distributing the literature in a small school may belong to the secretary, superintendent, or even the minister. It is an important work, however, and as soon as possible ought to be delegated to a "literature librarian." The literature librarian's work is as follows:

1. He first learns what type of literature has been selected for the school by the board of education, and from what publishing house it is to be ordered.

2. The librarian studies the catalog of the publishing house selected by the board of education and tells the departmental superintendents and teachers what lesson helps and other supplies are available. Publishers of Sunday-school supplies list these materials either as "periodical" or "merchandise" items. The periodicals are publications which appear regularly each week, month, or quarter. They may be lesson quarterlies, monthly or weekly magazines and papers, leaflets, and the like. Merchandise items include books, handwork supplies, visual aids, and many other things found in the catalog. A new catalog is published each year showing the new literature and supplies, changes in prices, and other information. It is the librarian's responsibility to have the latest catalogs and other descriptive material on hand so that all Sunday-school workers are fully informed of the teaching helps available.

3. At regular intervals, usually once a quarter, the librarian confers with the departmental superintendents and workers and makes up the order for teaching materials. Order blanks and detailed instructions for ordering are furnished by the publishers.

After the librarian makes out the school's order, he gives it to the superintendent, who checks it and perhaps discusses it with the board of education. Much care is taken to be sure that the order is complete and accurate. Sending additional orders and making changes in orders cause confusion and delay.

The librarian sends the order at least six weeks before the literature and supplies are needed by the school. This means that the librarian will begin to make out the order at least two months before the materials are needed. Ordering literature is an important responsibility, and it must be done correctly.

4. When the literature and supplies are received they become the immediate responsibility of the literature librarian, who opens them, arranges them for distribution, and keeps them available in a neatly arranged supply cabinet. At least two weeks before it is needed, the literature is given to the departments for which it was ordered. Then the department or class librarian assumes the responsibility for it. Each department should have its own supply cabinet or closet for storing literature and merchandise. From this cabinet the departmental librarian makes the distribution to the teachers and other workers who are to use the material.

Later, when discussing the school's equipment, we shall consider further these storage places for supplies, along with the work of the librarian who looks after the other items and equipment.

Secretarial and Bookkeeping Staff. Every Sunday school, regardless of size, needs three kinds of records.

1. *Enrollment.* When a person becomes a member of the school (usually attendance for three Sundays changes one from a "visitor" to a "member" of the Sunday school), he is enrolled. Enrollment cards may be purchased from publishers or a school may print its own. The card should show the date of enrollment, complete name of new member (correctly spelled), birth date (this may be the month and day of the year only for adults), complete and correct address, department to which the new member is assigned, church membership (if any), and similar information regarding other members of the family.

This enrollment card, or one that is kept with it, also shows the member's progress as he is promoted from one class or department to another. It is kept permanently in the files of the church, available to the minister, the committee on evangelism, board of Christian education, and other workers.

The enrollment secretary or an assistant also assigns pupils to the proper departments and classes and sees to it that they are escorted, introduced, and made to feel at home in the school.

2. *Attendance.* These records show the Sunday-by-Sunday attendance of every member, class, and department, and of the school as a whole. Printed attendance record books are available from the publishing houses or book stores. Securing the attendance statistics and recording them is the task of the secretarial and bookkeeping staff. The secretary also posts the amount of money received in the class, departmental, and school offerings. The treasurer is thus protected because he has a record of the money that is placed in his care. Such records are necessary whether the money goes into the general church funds or is kept in the school's treasury.

3. *Official Records of Meetings, and Correspondence.* These involve an entirely separate kind of secretarial work and may be assigned to someone besides the Sunday-school secretary. The records should be prepared to last indefinitely. Carbon copies are to be kept of all minutes of meetings and correspondence.

THE ESSENTIALS OF AN EFFICIENT RECORD SYSTEM

PUPIL

Necessary Information—Four Copies   Visitor Only ———

- Name
- Address
- Phone
- Birth Date
- Parents' Names
- Names and Ages of other members of the family   Church Relationship
- **Class Assigned to ———

ENROLLMENT DESK — GENERAL SEC.
Located in a good spot to receive all newcomers!

Pupil and Information

Information (Duplicate)

DEPARTMENT SUPERINTENDENT (Pupil and Duplicate)

TEACHER & CLASS (Pupil and Duplicate)

CHURCH OFFICE
- Family Record Card
- Visitation Evangelism Prospect Card
- Notify other classes of prospects in the family for their class.

MINISTER'S DESK
- Visitation Card

Week-by-Week Records in Every Class

Teacher's Own Class Book and Pupil Information Work Sheet
———————
Class Secretary

Individual Pupil Report Envelope
POINT SYSTEM
(Returned to the Bible-school Sec.)

GOAL: Active Church Membership

Pupils' Class Report Book for Bible-school Sec.

Notice of Absentee to Teacher & Supt.

Report on call

> Bible-school secretary will give detailed reports of attendance, new pupils, absentees, and Six-point System grade by class and for the total school.

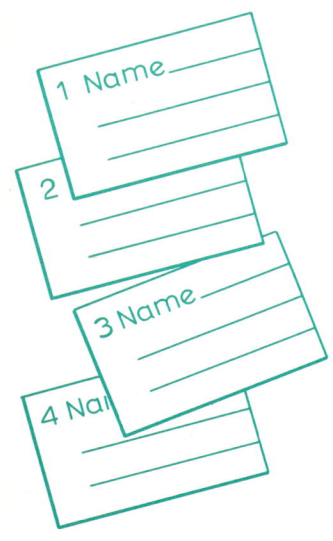

Leonard G. Wymore, executive secretary of the National Christian Education Convention, who devised the chart setting forth "The Essentials of an Efficient Record System," and gave permission for its use here, also made some suggestions concerning how to improve the records of a Sunday school. First, he lists "essential material needed as shown by the chart."

1. An enrollment desk and secretary in a prominent place where newcomers may be brought for enrollment.

2. Four copies of the information obtained at enrollment time, using different colored paper for each copy. One copy goes to the general superintendent, another to the departmental superintendent, the third to the enrollment secretary's file, and the fourth to the pupil.

3. Two class roll books or attendance check sheets for each teacher. One is to be returned to the secretary each Sunday and the other is for the teacher's use during the week.

4. Six-point envelope for each person, except pupils in the Primary Department and younger.

5. Absentee lists to be filled out and given quickly to all who are concerned.

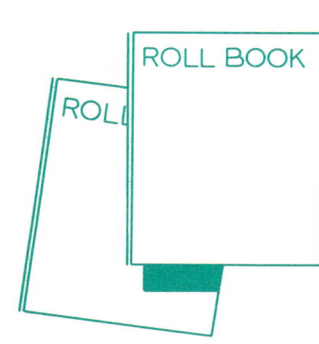

Next, Mr. Wymore tells "how to go about improving Sunday-school records."

1. Review the system now in use and learn where it needs to be improved.

2. Gather samples of record systems offered by various publishers and of those used in other schools.

3. Meet with your assistant superintendent, secretarial staff, and department heads to present the results of your findings. Do not decide yourself what is to be done, but let the entire group decide.

4. When you and this group decide upon the system to be followed, let the secretary present it to the entire body of officers and teachers and obtain their understanding and whole-hearted support.

Under another heading Mr. Wymore made another excellent suggestion. He said (and the capitals are his), "RECORDS MUST BE *USED* AND NOT JUST KEPT." You, the superintendent, can use the records in these ways:

Enrollment: The superintendent ought to be informed by the enrollment secretary of every new pupil enrolled in the school. He then sees to it that every newly-enrolled pupil is called upon in the home, by the teacher. From time to time the superintendent should also find out how many pupils are enrolled in each department and class.

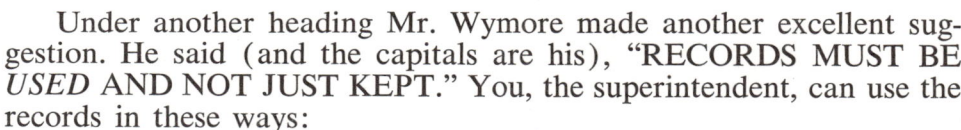

Attendance: Each Sunday the superintendent is informed of the attendance in each department, grade, or class. From time to time, perhaps once a month, he should be given a report of the average attendance for the month, quarter, or year of each department, grade, or class. In this way he can know how each group is progressing and can detect trouble spots where his help is needed.

Minutes: A carbon copy of the minutes of any meeting of Sunday-school workers is given to the superintendent so that he may see that proposed activities are carried out, proposed changes made, etc. He can also use the copy to help him plan for the next meeting.

Treasurer. Someone in every Sunday school must be responsible for receiving and recording the offerings, paying out the money as instructed, and keeping a record of such payments. This is true whether the money goes into a general church treasury or is placed in a separate Sunday-school fund. It is an important responsibility.

To protect the treasurer from any misunderstanding at any time, his books should be audited once each year. This auditing is done by comparing his receipts with the secretary's reports of offerings, and comparing the payments with those authorized by the school, as shown on the secretary's minutes and by receipts that have been given to the treasurer with payments. Those who make the audit may be any two or three businessmen or women. In large churches auditing firms are often employed. Whoever does the auditing reports to the supervising body, whether it be the general board of officers, the board of Christian education, or the Sunday-school workers' council.

Ushers. Ushering, even in the smallest Sunday school, is so important that it requires special attention. Greeting every arrival individually can make attendance an attractive and inviting experience. The superintendent should assign one or more persons to this responsibility, giving each a copy of these instructions:
1. Be the first to arrive on Sunday morning.
2. Be cheerful and helpful in attitude, neat and attractive in appearance, and polite and considerate in manner.
3. Offer to take visitors to the proper classes or to the enrollment secretary.
4. Introduce visitors to others who can then take the responsibility for them, seeing that they meet the department head or teacher directly interested in them.
5. Look after windows and doors, keeping them closed or open as needed.
6. Distribute songbooks, lesson leaflets, and other materials needed for the opening assembly program.

Instructive booklets on ushering may be purchased from the publishing house. Be sure to impress upon your ushers the importance of their responsibility.

HI-TEEN CLASS

Officers of Organized Classes. These are responsible to their classes who elect them but can also be important helpers to the general superintendent.

The class president and vice-president, if informed about the superintendent's program for the school year, can lead the class in helping it to succeed.

The class secretary and treasurer work with the school's secretary and treasurer to make the school function smoothly.

In some schools the officers of organized classes are invited to attend the superintendent's general conference of teachers and officers. The information they obtain there helps them to lead their classes in cooperating with the school's program. Class officers may also advance

in time to positions as teachers or officers in the school. The training they receive at the workers' conferences will be helpful for such advanced responsibility.

Secretaries of Special Activities. Listed below are committees for special activities which may have secretaries who are to report to the official church board.

1. Missions. The secretary of this commitee may have such duties as arranging for missionaries to visit and speak at special meetings of the church, corresponding with missionaries for news of the mission field, helping Sunday-school teachers emphasize missions in their classes, etc.

2. Temperance. The secretary of this committee can keep in touch with agencies that oppose traffic in alcoholic beverages, seeing that instruction is given in the classes and by posters, displays, exhibits, a reading table and library, dramatic presentation, and by many other means.

3. Recreation. Basketball, baseball, volley ball, and other types of sports may be a part of the church and Sunday-school program. The recreation secretary can also organize picnics, hikes, hayrides, tours of historic places, etc. for the various age groups in the church.

4. Visitation. The visitation secretary can help each department and older class of pupils devise a program of visiting the sick, absentees, prospective members, and others. Programs can be provided at homes for the aged, orphanages, jails, and elsewhere. Not only do the pupils participating in such activities do much for the Lord and His church, they also grow as Christians. In many rapidly growing Sunday schools the entire enrollment above the Junior Department is enlisted in a program of visitation, led by the teachers and officers.

5. Benevolence. Ministering to charity cases within and without the church, distributing food and clothing to the needy at Thanksgiving and Christmas and throughout the year are some of the many activities for which the secretary of the benevolence committee is responsible.

6. Greeting. This committee's secretary sends birthday, congratulatory, sympathy, and "get well" messages on behalf of the Sunday school.

Many other committees could be listed along with the duties of their secretaries, but these are the most common. Each secretary of these special activities is to be selected annually and installed in office with the other teachers and officers. Each secretary should have one or more assistants. The cost of activities is to be paid either by the Sunday school or from the general church treasury. All of these secretaries, as well as the other officers, are to be directly under the supervision of the general superintendent.

Where can you find teachers for your Sunday school? Read page 70 for the answer.

Can you name some of the questions on the teacher evaluation chart? You will find the chart on page 72.

Why is it a good practice to have each teacher evaluate himself at regular intervals? Page 71 will tell you the answer.

What three words summarize the qualifications of a good teacher? Can you elaborate on each word or qualification, telling why a teacher needs that certain thing? Turn to page 73 for the answers.

What three basic things can you do to fulfill your responsibilities toward your teachers? See page 74.

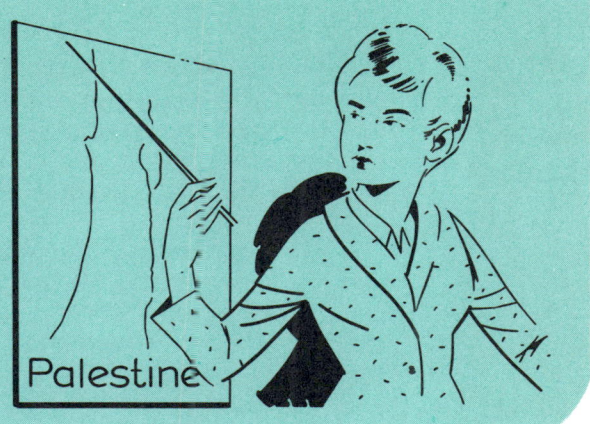

CHAPTER 8

YOU DEPUTIZE

teachers

Next Sunday several million consecrated men and women will stand before Sunday-school classes to teach portions of God's Word to the children, young people, and adults of America. They are the church's and the nation's greatest asset. They are the Sunday-school teachers. You have some of them in your school, under your supervision. To a great extent you are responsible for their success or failure.

SELECTING TEACHERS

Teachers are gifted by the Lord to do His work (Ephesians 4:11). He gives them specific orders to recruit people for Him and to conserve Christians for Him by their teaching (Matthew 28:19, 20). During His ministry on this earth He showed them by His example how and what they are to teach. He warns them to do their best.

God has published in one book, the Bible, the purpose and history of His plan for mankind. He has sealed it with the blood of His own Son, and has placed it in the hands of a person and called that individual "teacher." The teachers in your Sunday school are some of your deputies which are to help achieve the purpose of the school.

You do not select the teachers. This, according to the Bible, is the responsibility of the elders (or bishops, presbyters, or pastors, as they may also be called), for they are the overseers of the flock which is the local church. They are the ones which make up the greatest part, if not all, of the board of Christian education. They select the teachers. But they look to you for counsel and guidance. You, as superintendent, must know the qualifications and duties of the teachers. You, working through the departmental heads, direct the activities of the teachers.

In some schools there may be one or more classes that elect their own teachers each year, along with the class officers. This situation can be corrected by having the board of Christian education select the teachers, then notify the classes of the selections; each class may then wish to "elect" its teacher as a formal courtesy.

Teachers and more teachers are needed. Every class ought to have two teachers—one who teaches most of the time, or the Number One teacher, and another who serves as the assistant, substitute, or co-teacher. The latter, who may be referred to as the Number Two teacher, is trained and ready to step in and teach whenever the need arises. In addition to the two regular teachers for each class there should be "roving" teachers for emergency duty, supervisory teachers to help with the training, and teachers-to-be who are in training for future service.

Where can you find teachers? Right in your own school. Every adult in your school is a potential teacher. Older young people who have grown up in the Sunday school and church are also potential candidates for this important responsibility. Many teachers, perhaps most of them, began teaching in their teens. But there is a danger here to be avoided. Don't enlist a teen-ager just because he or she is willing. Young people need to mature before they are ready to teach.

Big businesses find their more important workers in schools. Capable men and women are sent to colleges and universities to interview graduates, to tell them of the opportunities available for careers, and to solicit their applications for jobs. The Sunday-school superintendent follows the same plan. His own school is the field where he finds teachers.

Louis Entzminger, a Sunday-school leader of an earlier generation, told in an article in *The Lookout* how he successfully enlisted teachers. In his day his methods were used to build twenty-three of the twenty-five largest Sunday schools in the United States. On one occasion, after presenting the need for teachers in a certain school, he gained the co-operation of a teacher of a young women's class which had forty members. The teacher told him, "In my class are thirty-nine young women whom I have been teaching for two years. Every one of them can teach. I will help you enlist them." Said Mr. Entzminger, "She helped us enlist every one of the thirty nine. They were not trained teachers, but the best way to train teachers is to enlist them, put them to teaching, and train them at the same time."

Mr. Entzminger went on to say that within three months the teacher who gave up thirty-nine members of her class of forty to the cause of teaching, could boast of a class of 150. Mr. Entzminger concluded, "Like John the Baptist, this teacher said, 'I must decrease, he (it—the Sunday school) must increase.' I could illustrate this truth time and again with similar stories."

All about us are multitudes of people who need to know Jesus. In every church there are those who can teach them. Your job, as superintendent, is to lead in bringing the unreached into your school and to provide them with capable teachers. The teachers can be found in the local church—people with unused talent for the Lord, now going to waste. Remember, however, that your program of teacher enlistment is not to be a one-time shot, nor an occasional spurt. It is to be a continuous effort, with the goal of improving the teaching in your school.

QUALIFICATIONS OF TEACHERS

To become a teacher in the Sunday school, more than a mere desire is required. While every church member is a potential teacher, not every person whose name is on the church roll is *qualified* to teach. It is necessary for you to have a thorough understanding of the qualifications of a good teacher before you begin to enlist new teachers. To help you understand these qualifications, evaluate the present teachers in your Sunday school. Prepare a check list by which the teachers can grade themselves. On the following page is a check-chart that you may wish to use. However, you may want to work out your own chart, with the help of the board of Christian education. Give one copy of the

chart to every teacher. Do not collect the charts again, but suggest that the teachers fill them out for their own benefits, learn their own weaknesses, and then work on improving themselves. Distribute other copies of the chart to the departmental superintendents. Each superintendent is to fill out a chart for every teacher in the department. When each chart is completed, it should be returned to you. After you have studied the charts, turn them in to the board of education. Remember, these charts are strictly for evaluating the *present* teachers of the Sunday school.

TEACHER EVALUATION CHART

	YES	NO
Is she (or he) an active, supporting member of the local church?		
Does she dress, speak, and behave in a way that brings honor to the Lord?		
Does she know and speak to each of her pupils by name?		
Does she visit in the home of each new pupil at once and in the homes of the others at regular intervals?		
Do good order and discipline prevail in her class?		
Is she faithful in attendance, always on time, with a well-prepared lesson?		
Does she use good grammar?		
Does she "talk the language" of her pupils, knowing and understanding their interests?		
Do her pupils respect her educational standing?		
Has her class increased its enrollment by at least ten per cent during the past twelve months?		
Does she promptly contact every absentee and bring him back to attend class regularly?		
Does she encourage her pupils to attend the other services of the church?		
Does she use a variety of methods in her teaching?		
Does she encourage pupil participation rather than doing all the talking herself?		
Does she keep her classroom neat and attractive?		
Does she take good care of the materials she uses so they can be used again?		
Is teaching in the Sunday school more important to her than anything else?		
Is she steadily improving instead of acting as though she has reached perfection as a teacher?		

The most important qualification of a teacher (or any Sunday-school worker) is the desire to improve. Possibly the worst affliction of the Sunday school and the entire church is pious self-satisfaction that stagnates the soul. If a church worker, or any Christian, is willing to study and strive for improvement, trusting the Lord for guidance, he can succeed. Before a person should be considered as a possible teacher in the Sunday school, even though he has been teaching for years, the willingness and desire to improve should be assured. What we are is God's gift to us. What we become, is our gift to Him.

What are the required qualifications for teachers? What have you the right to expect of them? We can boil the requirements down into three words:

1. *Ability*. A teacher must know three things: What he is to teach, whom he is to teach, and how to teach. In other words, he must be thoroughly familiar with the textbook of the Sunday school (the Bible), the age group of his pupils (their traits and characteristics), and the best methods for teaching that particular age group. As we stated in an earlier chapter, these three things can be summed up with these words:

    a. Theology
    b. Psychology
    c. Pedagogy

The able teacher must be a master of all three. This would be difficult indeed for an inexperienced, untrained person, were it not for the lesson helps available. The Bible teacher has more and better help than has the teacher of any other subject. The writers and editors of these materials are specialists in Sunday-school theology, psychology, and pedagogy. In the teacher's manual these three sciences have been employed in such a simple and effective way that the teacher can use them with ease. (Of course this fact does not relieve the teacher of studying.) A teacher's ability improves with training and experience, IF THE TEACHER IS CONSTANTLY STRIVING TO IMPROVE. You have the right to expect every teacher to do his best.

2. *Honesty*. You also have the right to expect the teacher to be honest with himself, his pupils, the church, and the Lord. If he is honest with himself, he will not indulge in habits or practices that will lower him in his own estimation. If he is honest with his pupils, he will arrive on time every Sunday with the lesson well prepared, ready to do his best to help the pupils grow as Christians. If he is honest with the church he will be an active supporting member of the local congregation and will place its interests ahead of his own. If he is honest with the Lord he will pray much, read the Bible regularly, study diligently, and strive always to improve—to be a workman approved by the Master.

3. *Teamwork*. The willing and consecrated teacher is a team worker. He co-operates in the program of the department, school, and church as a whole. He follows the line of organization, being willing to work under the departmental leader and others in supervisory positions. He attends departmental and general conferences and all services of the church. Sometimes a school must do without the services of a capable person because that person will not co-operate. A less capable person, but one who will co-operate, is preferred.

DUTIES OF TEACHERS

What are the duties of teachers? To teach, obviously. This teaching is a full-time, a twenty-four-hours-a-day, seven-days-a-week job. It is not limited to a brief half hour on Sunday morning. It includes active participation in the social activities of the class, a friendly interest in the well-being of each pupil, and exemplary conduct. A teacher teaches a little by what he says, more by what he does, and most by what he is. Actions speak louder than words. The teacher, therefore, must be present every Sunday, on time, with a Bible, an offering, and a well-prepared lesson. He must be present at every church service and activity as an example to his pupils. Your teachers should realize the importance of being good examples, as illustrated in this little story. A kindergarten child was downtown with his mother one day when he pointed to his Sunday-school teacher who was across the street, saying: "Look, Mother, there goes Mrs. God."

A library of books has been written about teaching in the Sunday school. These books have to do with the process of teaching mostly, yet they deal also with all the duties of the teacher. The superintendent will do well to read a book on teaching occasionally. It will help him to understand better the duties of the teachers.

YOUR RESPONSIBILITIES TOWARD YOUR TEACHERS

Your work with your church's board of education is to discover, select, and train teachers. But your responsibility toward them does not end when they are installed in their teaching positions. You must *encourage* them, *support* them, and *aid* them in every way you can.

To encourage teachers, the annual teacher-appreciation service, coupled with their installation, is recommended. Teachers may feel the importance of their jobs more if small signs are placed on their classroom doors showing their names, classes, and ages of pupils. Public and private words of commendation are always treasured by any person. Public prayers in the Sunday school can be encouraging to teachers if they include thanks to God for their work and petitions for divine help in their work. Some superintendents send birthday cards to all members of their staffs, writing on each a word of appreciation and praise.

To support your teachers, you must see to it that they are equipped with the best teaching aids available. "Nothing is too good for our teachers," ought to be your attitude. In addition to periodical literature, books, magazines, and other reading material, each teacher should have a chalkboard, flannelboard, and other helps. Take an interest in the classroom furniture and furnishings and see that each teacher has what is needed.

Other ways of aiding your teachers will come to your attention. Keep in mind your responsibilities toward them. Also keep in mind, however, that you are not the direct supervisor of the teachers, and that everything you say and do must be in such a way that it will not detract from the importance of the departmental superintendent.

What is the number one problem found in most churches? Read the first paragraph on this page. Is this the number one problem in your school?

Can you name the six general principles that you should know before you begin training Sunday-school workers? They are found on page 76.

What are the four basic or most common methods of training Sunday-school workers? Pages 76 and 77 list them for you.

Have you read page 78? If you have, then you should be able to name the three rules that you must follow if you wish to find the best workers available, and keep them at their jobs as long as they are the best workers.

CHAPTER 9

YOU DEPUTIZE

by training officers and teachers

Ask any minister or other experienced church worker to name the number one problem in the church and he will probably reply: "The need for better trained officers and teachers." This includes everyone, from the minister to the ushers, and from the musicians to the superintendent. Not one of us is as well trained as we should be. This fact is so well known that we need not discuss it further. (We may add, however, that workers in the Sunday school are better trained today than they have been at any time in the history of the Sunday school.)

Training the workers is a responsibility of the board of Christian education, but the superintendent is so directly concerned that he ought to know how this training is to be done, and have a leading part in it. He, or a secretary of training who reports to him and to the board of education, must keep a record of the training program. There should be a file of the entire staff, with a card or book page for each officer and teacher. This file is to show how much training each worker has completed. If there is a secretary of training, he or she can direct the training program and encourage the active participation of every worker. When the school year comes to an end, this secretary is to submit a report to the superintendent and board of Christian education showing the results of the training program.

Before we discuss in detail the various methods of training Sunday-school officers and teachers, let us consider some of the general principles:

1. *Consecration must come first.* A sincerely consecrated but untrained worker is more to be desired than a highly trained expert who is not consecrated. A truly consecrated person will be willing to train for improvement.

2. *Remember that the Sunday-school worker is a volunteer.* The public school can demand certain academic training of its teachers because it pays them a salary. The Sunday-school worker must be led to understand that his work is one of love—love for Jesus Christ and love for those who would know more about Him. His motive may at first be vague to him, therefore he must be carefully and patiently trained to understand his purpose as well as to know how to do his work. He cannot be ordered about as an employer would order an employee. He must be led to do his work as a servant of the Lord. This requires training.

3. *He does not have to be fully trained before he begins his work.* His best training will be his on-the-job experience. He ought to have the desired qualifications, however, and as much training in advance as possible.

4. *The training program is a continuous, permanent activity.* It is not merely an occasional "training course."

5. *Every worker must take part in this training.* No one, not even the minister, is ever as well-trained as he should be. The interest and enthusiasm of all workers are essential.

6. *The desire to improve and the willingness to study and work are required of every worker.* When one ceases to improve, he begins to fail. The church is handicapped by having incompetent workers who smugly and piously think they are doing well enough, and do not train to improve themselves.

The methods of training are many and varied. A church's training program may contain one or all of these methods. The more methods it uses, the better training it provides. The better the training, the better the school. Let us consider briefly each of the more common methods.

1. *Training courses.* There are many published training courses available. These courses cover every job in the Sunday school, telling how to do it. They also train the worker in the knowledge of the Bible, its contents and teachings. Inquiry at any Bible book store or publishing house will bring you complete details of these courses.

Many of the training courses offer credits to those who finish them satisfactorily. Some are included in a standard set up for the Sunday school.

Training courses may be studied in many ways. The occasional school of training for church workers, lasting several weeks with classes every night, is one method. Such a school can be conducted in the local church or by a group of churches in one community or area. Another method is to hold a weekly training class preceding the

Sunday evening church service, or on some evening during the week. It is becoming increasingly popular to conduct training classes as part of the regular Sunday morning school. Training courses may also be taken through correspondence with certain publishing houses. In such cases, qualified persons give the examinations to the trainees.

Some churches keep a library of training books available and encourage workers to study them. When the study is completed, an authorized training secretary or superintendent gives the examination. Because of its convenience and the fact that it provides a continuous, permanent program of training, this method shows a great deal of promise.

2. *Institutes, workshops, clinics, and laboratory schools* are regular events in some local churches or groups of churches. These may be held for a day or two, or they may extend over a period of a week or more. There are general sessions, in which all workers participate, and special classes for workers with special interests.

Workshops specialize in presenting the many methods of teaching.

Clinic sessions are those in which the work in the school is analyzed, in an effort to discover weaknesses and provide means for overcoming them.

Laboratory schools demonstrate Sunday-school work and discuss the methods demonstrated in an effort to make improvements.

Experienced specialists in the various fields of the Sunday school lead in the institutes, workshops, clinics, and laboratory schools. Sometimes these leaders are sent out by publishing houses to conduct these programs of Sunday-school improvement.

3. *Conventions and conferences* in county, state, and national form are held for Sunday-school workers. Most local churches participate in such conferences and conventions at least once a year. The superintendent of the Sunday school usually receives literature concerning such conventions and, in co-operation with the board of education. encourages the officers and teachers to attend. The spiritual uplift as well as the knowledge gained at such meetings helps the workers to do better in their jobs.

4. *On-the-job training*, sometimes called in-service training, provides continuous improvement for the worker. If he is the officer or teacher that he ought to be, he will learn by experience, and will use this learning to improve in his work. The teachers, for example, will find various methods of teaching suggested in their lesson manuals. By trying out these methods, and perhaps improving on them, the teachers improve themselves. There are several in-service training activities that the superintendent can direct.

One of these in-service training activities directed by the superintendent is the workers' conference. Although the conference is for planning progress and solving problems, its chief purpose is training

the workers. The "business session" should occupy about a half hour, while the "training session" ought to take a full hour.

Visiting other schools to observe their methods is good training. The superintendent ought to encourage Sunday-school workers to visit other schools while on vacation and ask them to report their observations to him. Perhaps the methods of other schools can be discussed in the workers' conferences to determine if they are better than those used in your school.

Encourage your Sunday-school workers to read books and articles that pertain to their particular jobs. Also encourage each person to build a library of his own, made up of books and magazines dealing with his work, whether it is teaching, planning programs, conducting a department, ushering, doing secretarial work, etc. In some churches these books are paid for out of the treasury with the understanding that they are to be passed along to each worker's successor.

Training of Sunday-school workers involves observation and supervision. The superintendent, for example, observes the work of his officers, supervises the work, and makes suggestions for improvement. The departmental superintendents observe the work of the teachers in their departments and discuss with the teachers ways in which they may improve their teaching.

These supervisors, including the general superintendent, need to keep one step ahead of their staff members. This does not mean that a superintendent must know more than the secretary about the secretarial work of the school. But he ought to know the importance of the secretary's work, what information is desired, and how this information is to be used. The departmental superintendent may or may not be a trained teacher, but ought to know enough about teaching procedures to discuss the teacher's work with understanding. This means that the supervisory workers—the members of the board of Christian education, the minister, superintendent and his assistants, and the departmental superintendents—need to be trained perhaps even more than the workers under them. They need to take training courses, attend conventions and conferences, read books and magazines, visit other schools and continually strive for improvement in their own school.

A superintendent cannot expect the workers in his school to study to improve themselves if he will not lead the way.

No statistics are available, but a general conclusion has been made that the average Sunday-school worker stays on the job about five years. This is not long enough. Since improvement comes with training and experience, the more a worker trains and the longer he serves, the better he can do his work. The goal, therefore, is to find the best person available for the job and keep him at it as long as he is the best person available. To do this, follow these three rules:
    1. Select workers carefully and prayerfully.
    2. Train them thoroughly and continuously.
    3. Show appreciation for their services.

What is an installation service for teachers and officers? After you have read this page, you will be able to answer this question.

Do you know what a teachers and officers appreciation service is? Read page 81.

What are some of the features that installation services and appreciation services should include? Why? If you have read this chapter, you will be able to describe these features.

Why are installation and recognition services important? Four reasons are listed on page 85.

What are some of the items that can be given for gifts at the recognition services? Suggestions are given on page 85.

CHAPTER 10

YOU DEPUTIZE

by rewarding officers and teachers

Appreciation of an officer or teacher begins with his appointment to a particular position. When he is informed about his selection for a certain job, he is to be carefully and thoroughly instructed as to its importance, its requirements, and his particular fitness for it. When he understands what the position involves, he accepts it, promising to perform his duties to the best of his ability.

Then comes an event that ought to mean a great deal to him as an individual and to the success of the entire school. This event is the public service in which he is installed in office as a teacher or officer. This installation service, if it is to be successful, should be as dignified and impressive as possible. It can be held at any time that is most suitable to your school and church. Many churches conduct it as a part of the Sunday morning worship program one Sunday each year. On that Sunday a special sermon is delivered, one that is appropriate to the occasion. Other churches set aside a Sunday evening once a year for such a service while others give banquets to honor the new officers and teachers and install them in office.

On the following page is the outline of a typical installation service. This program has been used annually by a large Sunday school in the midwest. Each time it is used it is printed in the church's Sunday bulletin or calendar so that all members of the congregation can read and understand clearly exactly what is taking place in the service. Being able to read the program as it progresses may serve to inspire men and women to become teachers and officers in the Sunday school also.

INSTALLATION SERVICE

Statement of purpose of this service by superintendent or minister

Leader: Do you, teachers and officers, gladly reaffirm your faith in, and loyalty to, Jesus Christ?

Teachers and Officers in unison: I readily desire to reaffirm my belief in Jesus Christ as the divine Son of the living God, and I am eager that my witness of loyalty to Him as Lord may be seen in my life as well as my words.

Leader: Will you, teachers and officers, reaffirm your faith in, and loyalty to, the Bible, God's holy Word?

Teachers and Officers in unison: It is my conviction that the Bible is the revelation of God's will to men through chosen spokesmen; that it is the power of God unto salvation to all who believe; that its truth is final and eternal and is the answer to all the needs of men and nations. I will so teach it in loyalty and conviction, so that others may hear the gospel.

Leader: Do you now reaffirm your faith in the church and your loyalty to it?

Teachers and Officers in unison: I believe that the church is the body of Jesus Christ, himself being the head and final authority. Since He loved the church and gave himself up for it, I shall love it dearly and make it first in my loyalty and concern. I shall do everything in my power, example, and influence to help those I teach to see that the purpose of the church's school is to enlarge and emphasize the God-given message and mission of the church. I shall myself be loyal to the services of worship.

Leader: Will the teachers and leaders of the children now state their pledge of loyalty and service?

Teachers and Officers of the Children's Division in unison: I believe my call to teach is from God who has committed to my care the molding and shaping of precious lives for a Christian destiny. I realize with concern that my actions and attitudes teach more to the children than even what I say and teach. I pray God to grant me wisdom to be and do and say only that which will make Jesus Christ, His Word and church appealing to the children I teach. I pledge myself to much study and prayer in order to accomplish my tremendous responsibility.

Leader: Will the teachers and leaders of the Youth Division now state their loyalty and purpose?

Teachers and Officers of Youth Division: Realizing that the youth I teach are the coming church and world of tomorrow and that they are now forming for life their beliefs, habits, and attitudes, I solemnly pledge myself to give my best in study, prayer, service, and life in order to help the youth I teach to develop into well-rounded, faith-filled Christians with deep convictions and great hearts of love and concern for Christ's church and His world-wide kingdom, for peace and brotherhood.

Leaders: Will the teachers and leaders of adults please state their pledge of purpose and loyalty?

Teachers and Leaders of Adults: I desire to accomplish four main objectives—the evangelism of the unsaved; the development of the individual Christian in the grace and knowledge of our Lord; the building of Christian homes; aiding my pupils to become citizens of real Christian influence in the world in which they live. To this end I pledge myself, asking God to sustain and empower me in accomplishing my task.

Prayer of Dedication.

APPRECIATION SERVICE

Along with the installation service, or on a separate occasion if desired, every church ought to hold an annual appreciation program for its workers. This may be as elaborate as you wish to make it. On the next few pages are some program outlines and other suggestions for use in planning a program of appreciation. Not all these suggestions can be used in any one program, of course. The planning committee, which may be the board of Christian education, may wish to use some of these suggestions as it plans the appreciation service.

BUILDERS FOR CHRIST

Teachers, officers, and their assistants are seated together and each is given a long-stemmed flower. A vase, which represents the church, is placed in a prominent place where it can be seen by everyone.

As each department is called, the teachers and officers stand while the leader reads the words of appreciation. Each worker is then introduced after which he or she places the flower in the vase while giving his response. This act is to represent the life of service each is willing to give to build Christ's church. This response should come from the heart, memorized if possible, and spoken clearly and with conviction. Be sure that the vase which is to be used is of suitable size to accommodate the number of flowers being used.

Hymn: "I Love to Tell the Story"

Leader: Recite following poem from memory, or read it with proper emphasis and expression:

BUILDING A TEMPLE

A builder builded a temple,
  He wrought it with grace and skill;
Pillars and groins and arches
  All fashioned to work his will.

Men said as they saw its beauty,
  "It shall never know decay.
Great is thy skill, O builder;
  Thy fame shall endure for aye."

> A teacher builded a temple
>   With loving and infinite care,
> Planning each arch with patience,
>   Laying each stone with care.
> None praised her unceasing efforts
>   None knew of her wondrous plan,
> For the temple the teacher builded
>   Was unseen by the eyes of man.
>
> Gone is the builder's temple,
>   Crumbled into the dust;
> Low lies each stately pillar,
>   Food for consuming rust.
> But the temple the teacher builded
>   Will last while the ages roll,
> For that beautiful, unseen temple
>   Is a child's immortal soul.

Leader: (To teachers and officers of the Nursery Department, children of ages 1, 2, and 3 years, naming teachers as they stand.) Just as you are the first to teach the children in the Bible school, so are you to be the first to speak words of self-dedication, and to add your tokens of consecration to this vase which represents Christ's church. (Note: Instead of calling the names of all teachers and officers at once, the leader may give the general words of introduction, then name each worker as he or she steps forward.)

Responses: As the teachers and officers step forward with their flowers, one at a time, each may quote an appropriate verse of Scripture, the last person closing with a sentence prayer of dedication instead of a quotation. Suggested quotations for the Nursery Department workers are these: Luke 2:10, 11; Luke 2:22; Luke 18:15a. Others may be found easily.

Leader: Teachers of the Kindergarten Department, we know that it requires patience and understanding as you work with our little ones in the Bible school. Their first impressions of Christ and His teachers are lasting ones. Therefore your responsibility is indeed great. Jesus said, "Suffer little children to come unto me, and forbid them not: for of such is the kingdom of God" (Luke 18:16b).

Responses: Luke 9:47, 48; Matthew 18:2, 3; Proverbs 22:6; etc.

Leader: Teachers and officers of the Primary Department, after the seed of Christianity is sowed in the hearts of our little children, the responsibility of nurturing and developing that precious seed falls into the hands of the Primary Department officers and teachers. Too often we fail to recognize the efforts of you who work so faithfully each Lord's Day. Jesus knew how teachable little children are when He said, "Whosoever shall not receive the kingdom of God as a little child, he shall not enter therein" (Mark 10:15). The beauty of childhood is reflected in the beautiful bloom you add to the vase.

Responses: 2 Timothy 3:15; Luke 18:17; Mark 10:16.

Leader: Teachers and officers of the Junior Department, the foundation of Christian living is laid in the hearts of men and women at an early age. Truly, "as a twig is bent so shall it grow." Great are your responsibilities and privileges as you continue to shape the lives of our boys and girls who are yet at such a teachable age. Just as the flowers you hold are needed in the vase, so are the flowers of childhood needed in Christ's church.

Responses: Matthew 5:6; James 2:17; James 3:1; Proverbs 20:11, and other appropriate Scriptures.

Leader: Teachers and officers of the Junior High Department, what a debt we owe you. As a rule men and women do not understand boys and girls in their early teens. Boys and girls must be always busy or their attention is lost. When Jesus was twelve, He sat among the learned men of that day both hearing them and asking them questions. Just as you are adding beauty to this flowering vase. so you are adding immeasurably to the beauty of the church through your faithful teaching of this very important age.

Responses: Luke 2:42-46; Luke 2:49-52; James 1:17; Proverbs 19:18, etc.

Leader: Teachers and officers of the Senior High Department, your pupils are at the age when one is neither child nor adult, when life holds great expectations and uncertainty. The importance of Christian teaching at this age cannot be overestimated. As boys and girls approach the fascinating age of youth may they, with your help, like Jesus, increase in wisdom and stature and in favor with God and man. As you place your flowers in the vase we feel deep gratitude for your efforts.

Responses: 2 Timothy 2:15; James 1:5; James 1:12, and other appropriate verses.

Leader: Teachers and officers of the Young People's Department, your pupils are at the age when they live in two worlds at once: the world within and the world without. The world without exerts a tremendous pressure. As a class, young people at this age are by nature impelled toward the making of a home and the founding of a family of their own. This homing tendency is one of the greatest safeguards to civilization, and one of the most divine of human impulses. All Bible teachings concerning the home and family are not only inspiring, but interesting. Jesus held the family in such high regard that He built His church according to family ideals. The family is a sacred institution. Young men and young women are interested in the teachings of God's Word upon all phases of this subject. There is no correction of the divorce evil except the adoption of the family ideals found in the New Testament. The teachers of this age group all have the responsibility to teach and guide our young people so that they can resist the pressures of outside influences and cling to sane, clean Christian living. As you add your flowers to the others we pray that you will be divinely guided as you teach this important age group in our Sunday school.

Responses: 1 Timothy 4:12; 1 Timothy 6:12; Proverbs 22:1; Proverbs 22:5; Ecclesiastes 12:1; 2 Timothy 2:22.

Leader: Teachers and officers of the Adult Department, you teach those pupils who are the backbone of the present church. Among these classes are the members of the official board, Sunday-school

teachers and officers, mothers, fathers, and grandparents. The ages range from young manhood and womanhood to those who have passed the honored threescore and ten mark. Church goers of this age are eager to learn more and more. We know much preparation must be made in order to present interesting lessons each Lord's Day. There is no better way to prepare yourself than to make a careful study of Christ as teacher. He is not only the Jesus of history, but He is the cosmic Christ who is adequate for all time. He knew the holy Scriptures. He placed the divine Word in a category by itself. He made the sacred writings the basic subject of His teaching so that the people pressed upon Him to hear the Word of God. He commended the Scriptures to others as the infallible rule of faith and practice. In speaking of them He said: "They are they which testify of me" (John 5:39). The adult teachers have the authority of Christ behind them for He said: "Go teach" with the promise, "Lo, I am with you alway." Remember His words as you add your flowers to our bouquet.

Responses: Matthew 7:28, 29; 2 Timothy 3:16, 17; Titus 1:9; Hebrews 5:12; Titus 2.

Leader: Now we come to a most important group—the officers of the Sunday school. Here are the architects, the planners, managers, supervisors of the church's Sunday morning school. As we introduce each of them personally, let us remember the long hours of hard work, the seasons of prayer, the continuous study required to lead in this important task. (The leader introduces in turn, with an appropriate word about each, the superintendent, assistant superintendent, the musicians, secretaries, treasurer, librarian, departmental superintendents, activity secretaries and any other officers your Sunday school might have.)

Responses: Ephesians 4:11, 12; Ephesians 4:13; Ephesians 4:14; Ephesians 4:15; Ephesians 4:16; John 6:45; Romans 10:17; Romans 12:2; Romans 12:9; Romans 12:10; Romans 12:11; Romans 12:12; Romans 12:13; Romans 12:21; 1 Corinthians 14:12; 1 Corinthians 14:40, etc.

Leader: As our bouquet is completed, let us add that officers, teachers, and class members are needed to complete the work Christ left for us to do. May we all be faithful to the task that we may say with confidence, as did our Saviour to our heavenly Father: "I have glorified thee on the earth: I have finished the work which thou gavest me to do" (John 17:4).

Solo: "My Task" or some other appropriate hymn.
Prayer of Dedication and benediction, with all present singing as a prayer response, "Have Thine Own Way, Lord."

Closing Hymn: "Onward Christian Soldiers" (by entire congregation).

In addition to the hymns mentioned in the program on the last few pages you can use any of the following hymns in your appreciation services: "Joyfully Serving the King," "Help Me Find My Place," "It Pays to Serve Jesus," "I Love to Tell the Story," "Living for Jesus," "A Charge to Keep," "Lead On, O King Eternal," "Tell Me the Story of Jesus," "Stepping in the Light," and "I Would Be True."

Below is a recitation that is very appropriate for both installation and appreciation services.

THE CHRIST

The greatest teacher of all time—who, with His original twelve disciples—has carried His teachings of brotherly love to all mankind throughout all corners of the world for nearly twenty centuries.

Here is a man who was born in an obscure village, the child of a peasant woman. He grew up in another obscure village. He worked in a carpenter shop until He was thirty, and then for three years He was an itinerant preacher.

He was nailed to a cross between two thieves. His executioners gambled while He was dying for the only piece of property He had on earth—and that was His coat. When He was dead He was taken down and laid in a borrowed grave through the pity of His friend.

Nineteen wide centuries have come and gone and today He is the centerpiece of the human race and the leader of the column of progress.

I am far within the mark when I say that all the armies that ever marched, and all the navies that were ever built, and all the parliaments that ever sat, and all the kings that ever reigned, put together have not affected the life of man upon this earth as powerfully as has that ONE SOLITARY LIFE.—*Hoffman.*

Gifts should be given to all officers and teachers at each appreciation service. Each gift may be small such as a flower, certificate, or award pin. Or you may wish to give more expensive gifts, such as appropriate books, Bibles or New Testaments, etc. In some schools the pupils in each class contribute money for the gifts of appreciation.

An annual installation and recognition service is desirable for four reasons:

1. It elevates the teaching function to its proper place in the church.
2. While the teachers' and officers' satisfaction comes mainly from serving the Lord, public appreciation gives them encouragement.
3. It inspires the teachers and officers to improve.
4. It leads others in the church to think, "I would like to be a worker in the Sunday school."

Section 4

you supervise

Chapter 11—Yourself
    How to Measure Up Spiritually
    Are You Physically Fit?
    Yours Can Be a Pleasing Personality
    The Secret of an Improved Mind

Chapter 12—Your Workers
    Supervising Your Officers
    Supervising Your Teachers

Chapter 13—Workers' Conferences
    What Is a Workers' Conference?
    How to Make It Work

Chapter 14—Pupils
    The Six-point Plan
    Organized Classes
    Discipline Is No Problem If You Know How

Chapter 15—Attendance
    Seven Rules for Building Attendance
    Methods of Recruiting
    Rescue That Absentee!
    Methods of Conservation

Chapter 16—Equipment
    A Look at the Building
    A Peek into the Classrooms
    Furnishings Are Important

Chapter 17—Financing
    How to Take up Offerings
    Be Careful! You Are Using God's Money
    The Budget

In what four ways should a good Sunday-school superintendent try to improve? You will know after you have read this page.

What are some of the things that make up physical fitness? Why should a superintendent be physically fit? Read pages 91 and 92.

Name some of the qualities that help to make up a good personality, and one that is becoming to a superintendent. These qualities are listed in the personality profile test on page 93.

Can you name some of the many dangers of which a superintendent should beware? Pages 95 and 96 describe some of these dangers.

CHAPTER 11

YOU SUPERVISE

yourself

So far we have been talking mostly about your staff and faculty. We said that the most important qualification each of your workers must have is the desire to improve. This statement also applies to you. If you are willing and eager to improve you can be a good superintendent. If you think you "know it all" and are satisfied with yourself, you are not a good superintendent and will not become one until you change your attitude.

Your job is to supervise. The dictionary says a superintendent is one who supervises, one who has the oversight or direction of some work, enterprise, establishment, or institution. You are the superintendent of the most important enterprise in the world—the Lord's church, in its work of teaching. The public-school superintendent is the head of an institution that produces good citizens for the community, state, and nation. Your school is to produce good citizens for the kingdom of God. Much more could be said, but you get the point. Yours is a most important job. If you are worthy of it, you will want to do the best job possible.

So that you can be a successful superintendent, begin by making an analysis of yourself. Jesus, we learn from Luke 2:52, advanced in four ways. As His worker and servant, why not make a four-way check to see how you measure up to His pattern of improvement: spiritually, physically, socially, and mentally. The following pages contain suggestions and charts to help you see where and how you need to improve yourself so that you will be not only a better Christian, but a good superintendent of your church's Sunday school. Be sure to use every chart.

HOW TO MEASURE UP SPIRITUALLY

Asked to serve as superintendent of a Sunday school a man said, "I am not good enough." He was right. As Paul said in Romans 3:23, "All have sinned and come short of the glory of God." But the man who said, "I am not good enough," has the right beginning. He realized spiritual improvement was needed. If he was willing to strive for that improvement, he would be started on the way that leads to becoming a good superintendent.

What spiritual qualifications ought the superintendent to have? How can he improve himself spiritually? The Bible tells us we are to be "growing" as Christians. How does one grow as a Christian? The following check-chart will offer suggestions.

	YES	NO
Am I a professed Christian? That is, am I an active, supporting member of my local church?		
Do those in my home and at my work consider me to be the kind of Christian I ought to be?		
Do I pray frequently and at length about my work as superintendent?		
Do I read from the Bible every day and meditate on what I have read?		
Do I make it the rule of my life to attend all the services of the church?		
In public are my dress, words, and general behavior such as bring honor to my Lord?		
Am I thoroughly committed to the Christian work entrusted to me, willing to make the sacrifices necessary for success?		
In my innermost soul, and before God, am I absolutely sure that I am all that a Christian should be?		

Beware of that final question! It has a catch to it. No Christian is absolutely sure that he is all a Christian should be. The test of his sincerity, as has been said, is his determination to improve. Several goods ways to improve are suggested by the other questions. Frequent prayer, daily Bible reading and meditation, and faithful attendance at all the church's services will help to strengthen you spiritually.

If you are to help develop Christian character in the workers and pupils in your school, you must possess in your own life those characteristics which you desire to develop in others. Following are some questions designed to help you judge your Christian character. What are your strong qualities? What are your weaknesses? Check those where improvement is needed.

Are You . . .	*Or Are You . . .*
1. Open-minded, inquiring?	Narrow, dogmatic, not hungry for truth?
2. Accurate, thorough, discerning?	Indefinite, superficial, lazy?
3. Judicious, balanced, fair?	Prejudiced, led by likes and dislikes?
4. Original, independent, resourceful?	Dependent, imitative, subservient?
5. Decisive, possessing convictions?	Uncertain, wavering, undecided?
6. Cheerful, optimistic?	Gloomy, pessimistic, bitter?
7. Amiable, friendly, agreeable?	Rebellious, anti-social, disagreeable?
8. Democratic, sympathetic?	Snobbish, self-centered?
9. Tolerant, generous with a sense of humor?	Dogmatic, intolerant, selfish?
10. Kind, courteous, tactful?	Cruel, rude, untactful?
11. Tractable, co-operative, teachable?	Stubborn, not able to work with others?
12. Executive, forceful, vigorous?	Uncertain, weak, not capable?
13. Modest, self-effacing?	Egotistical, vain, autocratic?
14. Courageous, daring, firm?	Overcautious, weak, vacillating?
15. Honest, truthful, sincere?	Dishonest, hypocritical?
16. Patient, calm, equable?	Irritable, excitable, moody?
17. Regular, punctual, dependable?	Tardy, usually behind time, undependable?
18. Methodical, logical?	Haphazard, inconsistent?
19. Poised, erect in posture?	Ill-at-ease with poor posture?
20. Constant and earnest in prayer?	Cold, formal, negligent in prayer?
21. Feeling a religious certainty?	Under conflict, strain, uncertainty?

YOU SUPERVISE

22. Expanding your religious life? | Static in your spiritual life?
23. Desiring to win others to Christ? | Little concerned for the lost?
24. Interested in the Bible? | Little concerned about God's Word?
25. Deeply confident in the Bible? | Doubtful of portions of God's Word?
26. Fully consecrated to the Lord? | Reserving part of your life for yourself?
27. At peace with God? | Unrepentant?
28. Born again? | Not really converted?

Do not be discouraged by the realization that you are weak in many of the attributes listed. An honest appraisal of one's weaknesses is the first step toward improvement. The test, however, is not whether you are honest in realizing your weaknesses, but whether you are willing to undertake the rigorous program of self-improvement. In this, as in all things worthwhile, the Lord will help. May He bless you as you look to Him for that help.

ARE YOU PHYSICALLY FIT?

Jesus, the lad, "increased . . . in stature." He grew physically. You may be fully grown in a physical sense, but fitness involves more than height, weight, or age. It includes appearance, living habits, and the recognition that your body is the temple of the Holy Spirit.

Physical fitness is important. All will agree that illness, deformity, or other physical handicaps do not lower people in the esteem of the Lord or their fellow men. Nor should such handicaps keep us from serving in the church. Such abnormal and unusual limitations can interfere, however, with one's serving as Sunday-school superintendent

The superintendent is a public figure. He is observed, even though he may often have someone else appear for him in public. For that reason, he should be fit physically

His task is an exacting one, requiring attention seven days a week if it is to succeed. A body that is not well cannot endure the strain.

Proper appearance is desirable. A superintendent does not have to be handsome, or even good looking, to succeed. But his appearance should be attractive. Before appearing in public you should be clean-shaven, with your hair combed, have teeth clean and well-cared for; clothing neat, clean, and in good taste; shoes shined, etc. Is your posture erect? The way the superintendent stands, sits, and walks is an indication not only of whether he is physically fit, but of whether he is poised and self-confident.

NOT THIS--

BUT THIS!

Unusual and eccentric appearance is out of place for a superintendent. If a man wishes to grow a beard when beards are not common, he should forego the desire if he is a Sunday-school superintendent. His aim is not to attract attention to himself, but to the Lord.

I recall a superintendent who presided at a Sunday-school opening assembly one time, wearing a short-sleeved, open-necked shirt of transparent cloth. Plainly visible in both pockets were packages of cigarettes. He was a factory worker, who lived in the workingman's district of a factory town. But that did not excuse his carelessness, nor the harm he was doing to the work of the Lord.

As you stand before the mirror on Sunday morning, ready to go to Sunday school, check this list:

I am physically fit in the following respects:	YES	NO
My body is bathed and clean		
My hair is well-groomed		
My teeth and my breath do not offend		
My fingernails are trimmed and clean		
My clothing is clean, neat, and in good taste		
My shoes are well-heeled, soled, and shined		
There is nothing in my pockets that would offend my Lord or His people		

YOURS CAN BE A PLEASING PERSONALITY

"And Jesus increased . . . in favour . . . with man." How well do you get along with people? The superintendent must be an expert at getting along with people. Sociability is an art. To get along with other people in a friendly, helpful way, does not come naturally. To master the art, one must learn the fundamental principles, then practice ceaselessly.

On the next page is a personality profile test. Use the test honestly to see if your personality is all that it should be to help you succeed in your job as superintendent. Make a note of your weaknesses. Then strive diligently to overcome them.

Do not be discouraged if your grade on the test is low. Few people are *superior*, and not many are even *average* in all the personality traits listed in the test. To become average and eventually superior in these traits you will have to devote yourself to much careful study and practice.

PERSONALITY PROFILE TEST

For the Sunday-school Superintendent

QUALITY	DEFINITION	MY ESTIMATE LOW AVERAGE HIGH				
		1	2	3	4	5
Spirituality	Christianity, always putting God first					
Sincerity	Truth and genuineness					
Dependability	Loyalty, reliability, promptness					
Enthusiasm	Keen interest, zeal, earnestness					
Co-operation	Ability to work with others					
Self-confidence	Feeling sure your ability is equal to demands					
Well-groomed Appearance	Properly dressed and clean					
Good Health	Good physical condition					
Forcefulness	Using firm and decisive action and expression; not hesitant					
Emotional Stability	Ability to maintain poise at all times, even under emotional stress					
Tact	Saying and doing what is effective without offending					
Courtesy	Being polite, kind, considerate					
Friendliness	Cordial, sympathetic					
Persistence	Ability to continue effectively even with strong opposition					
Patience	Being long-suffering					
Use of Good English	Using words effectively in clear, understandable, correct grammar					
Pleasing Voice	Strong, rather low pitched voice, easily heard, but not irritating					

THE SECRET OF AN IMPROVED MIND

"And Jesus increased in wisdom." The secret of an improved mind is not how much natural intellectual ability you have. Nor is it simply education, which is acquired by study, research, and experimentation. You have often heard the term, "An educated fool."

Wisdom is one's willingness to learn and to keep on learning. "A wise man will hear, and will increase learning," we read in Proverbs 1:5. But verse seven adds, "fools despise wisdom and instruction."

A wise superintendent will use his intellect to increase his knowledge. Then he will strive for wisdom by learning to use that knowledge correctly. A good synonym for wisdom is "common sense." Of course every superintendent ought to have common sense. So one of your goals is to increase in wisdom. To begin, answer "yes" or "no" to the questions on the chart below.

Study each statement carefully then check—	YES	NO
1. I believe that an educated Sunday-school superintendent will do a better job than one who is not educated.		
2. I believe that the superintendent who ceases to learn will cease to serve acceptably.		
3. I believe that the Sunday school is more important than the public school and that its teachers ought to be as well-educated as those in the public school, even though I place public school education in high esteem.		
4. Academic training is not as important as spiritual living, but a successful superintendent ought to have both.		
5. I am always wise in making use of the knowledge which I have.		
6. I can name at least five dangers which confront me as a Sunday-school superintendent and tell how to avoid them.		
7. I regularly read at least one magazine that is published to help me in my work as superintendent.		
8. I have my own library of books, or access to one, that deal with the Sunday school.		
9. I attend conventions, conferences, workshops, etc., in an effort to find help in becoming a better superintendent.		
10. I am acquainted with a public-school principal and talk with him about my work as superintendent of a Sunday school.		

The statements on the check-chart are not intended to be complete. Many others could be given. These, however, are worth discussing briefly.

1. All else being equal, no one will deny that an educated superintendent will do a better job than one who is not educated. Surveys have been made to learn about Sunday-school teachers. These show that the average teacher is a high school graduate who has had one year of college training. No doubt the average Sunday-school superintendent is equally educated.

2. The superintendent who ceases to learn cannot expect to lead others in studying to learn.

3. The high standards in public education are resulting in a demand that workers in the Sunday school be better educated than in the past. One reason the educational level of the Sunday-school worker has not been emphasized is that the work is not professional. Unlike the public school, where the principal is paid a salary and is required to have certain academic training, the Sunday-school superintendent is neither paid nor required to have formal higher education.

This volunteer status of the Sunday-school superintendent does not mean that he is to be untrained. But his aptness for the job is measured in ways other than the amount of education he has had. His spiritual status, for instance, is far more important than whether or not he is a college graduate. His ability to get along with people is also an important factor to be considered. It would be a sad mistake if only those with certain college credits were selected to work in the Sunday school. However, every superintendent should try to acquire as much education as possible, along with the ability to use his knowledge wisely.

To emphasize this point, consider some reasons that your work is more important than that of workers in the public school.

Your purpose is more important. The public school helps the pupil to live better here on this earth. The Sunday school helps him to live a better life both here and in the next world.

Your source material is more important. The Bible is not only the world's best seller among books, it is the world's most important textbook, for it is the Word of God, the revelation of His will for man.

Your teachers are more important. They deal in eternal values, with the souls, as well as the minds and bodies of their pupils.

Your responsibility is greater. If a pupil in the public school fails to learn, he pays the penalty only during this life. If your school fails, the pupil may be lost eternally.

4. This statement has already been discussed, and is one with which everyone should agree.

5. Whoa! No, you are not always wise in making use of the knowledge which you have. You probably are like the farmer who was being

admonished by the county agricultural agent. Said the agent, "You could increase your crops, and improve your land if you would only learn the latest methods of farming." Answered the farmer, "Trouble with me is, I don't use half the learnin' I already have." All of us need to learn the latest methods in Sunday-school work, and we also need to apply those methods.

6. Five dangers? There are a hundred. Many have been mentioned already in this chapter. There are many more. Here are a few of the most common dangers:

Complacency. A superintendent is tempted to coast along "letting things ride," "taking it easy," instead of setting goals for improvement and then working to attain those goals.

Forgetting the individual. A superintendent must beware lest he think only of the school as a whole and forget the individual workers and pupils. Each is important. He must strive to know each one personally, particularly the workers, and to treat them as individuals and not as a group.

Vagueness of purpose. Ask the successful superintendent, and he can tell his school's attendance goal for next Sunday and what plans have been made for achieving that goal. He is equally able to tell of other plans for improvement.

Procrastination. This is a big word which means unnecessary and harmful delay. It is a common ailment, and Sunday-school superintendents especially need to be aware of it as a dangerous thing to be avoided.

Tolerance. This is a desirable trait in some ways, but not in all. For example, the superintendent must never say, "I know this is not good enough, but it is the best we can do." If he knows that "it" is not good enough, whether "it" be methods or equipment, he ought to be planning and working for improvement.

Prejudice. The superintendent must have an open mind and not rely on unfavorable opinions already formed.

Boastfulness. This is a sign of ignorance, as is the tendency to be argumentative. The wise superintendent avoids these dangers.

Growing stale. The superintendent should beware of growing stale. If you feel that you are, the best solution is to work hard until your enthusiasm is returned.

Numbers seven through ten on the chart are self-explanatory. Remember, if you are going to supervise others, you must first learn to supervise yourself. As Aesop's fable puts it, "Do but set the example yourself, and I will follow you. Example is the best precept." If you are a good superintendent, your workers will follow your example.

Can you give four reason why running a Sunday school is more important than running a home, school, business, etc.? These reasons are listed on this page.

Do you know the superintendent's "ten commandments"? Pages 98 through 100 list them for you. They are very important in your work of supervising all your workers, especially your officers.

Can you give the four-way formula for solving teacher problems? The formula is given on page 100.

How can you use the formula to help you solve the problem of the elderly, incompetent teacher? How will it help you to solve the problem of the unco-operative teacher? Read page 101.

CHAPTER 12

YOU SUPERVISE

your workers

Now that you have learned how to supervise yourself as a Sunday-school superintendent, let us turn our attention to your task of supervising your staff of officers and teachers. Running a Sunday school is not like running a home, or a business, or a public school, or a government, or anything else for that matter. Why? The reasons are listed below.

1. Running a Sunday school is more important. Your goal is an eternal one. It is not for this life only.

2. It is more difficult. You must supervise volunteer workers who are not compelled by law or by salary, but by their love for God and their neighbors.

3. It is intermittent, broken off and resumed again fifty-two times a year. You do not have the advantage of daily routine as in the home, school or business.

4. No training on the part of your workers is compulsory. Such training is urged, because it is important. But you cannot *require* or *demand* a worker to read a book, attend a training class, etc., if he does not want to do it.

You have one great advantage, however. You are doing the Lord's work, and your fellow workers are Christians who love the Lord and are dedicated to doing His will. You are divinely favored by having as your fellow workers the very best people in the community. More than that, the Lord is with you, to comfort, guide, and strengthen you. You have only to be true to Him and to His way, and you cannot fail.

There are two principal groups in your school—the workers and the pupils. You are responsible for helping each person in these two groups to do what is expected of him. We will discuss your supervision of the pupils more fully in another chapter.

Your workers are also divided into two groups—officers and teachers. The officers are under your DIRECT supervision while the teachers are under your INDIRECT supervision. Let us consider briefly your supervision of each group.

SUPERVISING YOUR OFFICERS

TEN COMMANDMENTS

Each member of your staff of officers is your personal responsibility. You may not be directly responsible for the teachers, as the board of Christian education and the departmental superintendents must choose and direct them. You may not be directly responsible for the pupils, who are under the supervision of the teachers. But you are the one and only supervisor of the assistant superintendent, musicians, departmental superintendents, secretaries, treasurer, ushers, librarian, and any other staff members that you may have.

We have already discussed their duties, selection, and training. What then, you may ask, is left to discuss? Just this: you must not only tell them what their duties are and see that they are trained for their jobs, but you must see that they follow instructions; and you must keep them working happily and faithfully. These tasks are not easy. They require a great deal of effort. No one is a born supervisor. So you must learn how to supervise and carry out these tasks. To help you, there are ten rules for good supervision listed on the next few pages. We might call them the superintendent's "ten commandments."

1. *Thou shalt remember thy purpose.* Your purpose has been discussed at length. It is a high one, the highest any man can have. If you pause to ask yourself, "What am I trying to accomplish?" the answer will help to keep you on the right track.

2. *Thou shalt consult thy guidebook.* Jesus gave you your job. He also gave you a guidebook, which tells you how you are to do your job. He would have been less than perfect, wouldn't he, if He had given you something to do and then neglected to tell you how to do it? The New Testament is a master book of good management and supervision. It has the solution for every kind of problem you will ever be called upon to solve.

3. *Thou shalt be no respecter of persons.* Remember from your school days the term "teacher's pet"? A supervisor has no pets. He honestly treats everyone the same. He is sincerely interested in the progress of each person. The newest comer is entitled to as much consideration as is your long-time friend. God is no respecter of persons. Let us follow His example.

4. *Thou shalt follow the line of organization.* Once a superintendent boasted to me, "I get along fine with the teachers. When I offer suggestions to them, they agree with me." He was promptly

asked, "What right do you have offering suggestions to the teachers? Your place is to offer suggestions, if you have any, to the department heads. They will pass your suggestions along to the teachers." When a superintendent bypasses one of his associates, he discourages that person, perhaps offends him, and weakens the organization.

5. *Thou shalt be a salesman.* One of your jobs is to make people WANT to do better work. That is the first rule of selling—to make people want what you have to sell. To do this, you must be able to understand the other person's point of view and look at certain things through his eyes, instead of just your own. For example, people will not become enthusiastic about neatness in classrooms and offices merely because you demand neatness. You must "sell" them on the fact that good housekeeping helps to create the right atmosphere and impression with their pupils. Point out also that it attracts attention to them, the workers, as *good* workers. Even though you have the authority to ask people to do things, it is worth taking the time to show them that what you want them to do is sensible, reasonable, and in their own, as well as the school's, interests. That is what makes the difference between grudging compliance and active co-operation.

6. *Thou shalt outline thy goals thoroughly, then coach thy associates in helping achieve them.* The best way to keep a greyhound running is to keep a rabbit right in front of his nose. You cannot trust a greyhound's memory or imagination. People need the same kind of stimulating supervision. First discuss with them the details of a particular task you want them to do. Ask for their opinions. Get them to make suggestions. Encourage them to feel as if the task is as much theirs as it is yours. Make certain they understand exactly what is to be done, how it is to be done, and who is to do it. Then keep the "rabbit" under their noses.

7. *Thou shalt give attention to details.* Success or failure in reaching a goal set for your Sunday school depends upon attention to details. Never take for granted that people know what to do, how to do it, or why they are doing it. Keep reminding them by advising them of the progress being made. Help the officers to see the importance of the background attention to details, as plans are carefully considered for every area of the Sunday School.

8. *Thou shalt look before leaping.* Before you begin a project, no matter what it is, consider all the factors involved, talk with others about the project, and then decide whether or not to go ahead with it. Once you make your decision to begin a project, then you may "leap"; but do it carefully, painstakingly, perseveringly, and prayerfully.

9. *Thou shalt remember the divine dignity of human personality.* Human beings are not tools or machines. Each is a creation of God, made in God's own image, and so precious to Him that He gave His only Son to die for that human being. Your associates in the Sunday school are priceless possessions. Love them. Esteem them highly. Praise their good works. Go out of your way to give utmost consideration to their wishes. Try hard to understand their viewpoints. Win their co-operation by your sincere thoughtfulness.

10. *Thou shalt expect criticism and profit by it.* Promoting an employee into a supervisory position, an employer wisely said, "From the time your promotion is announced, you will be under attack. A man cannot raise his head above the ramparts without being the target of snipers. The test of your ability will be whether or not you can take criticism, think it over, and use it if it is helpful." This is good advice for the Sunday-school superintendent. Expect criticism; and, if you can, use it to help you improve.

SUPERVISING YOUR TEACHERS

"How can you dismiss an elderly teacher who is no longer competent?"

"We have a teacher who will not attend the workers' conferences. Should the teacher be replaced?"

"One of our teachers is habitually late. What action should be taken?"

"A teacher of boys in our school is a cigarette smoker. What ought we to do about it?"

On and on go the complaints and requests for help in dealing with "problem teachers." What is the superintendent to do? We repeat: he is not directly responsible for the teachers. The departmental superintendents are responsible. If they cannot solve their problems, they come to you, the superintendent. You, in turn go to the board of Christian education.

This process may not be as simple as it sounds, however. Here is what actually happens: A departmental superintendent comes to you with a problem, expecting you to suggest a solution to that problem. If you can, fine. If you cannot, then you must take the problem to the board of education. The board will immediately ask you what you recommend. You are the man in the middle. You cannot say, "Don't ask me; that is your responsibility." You must know exactly what to do.

Most teacher problems can be solved by the application of a four-way formula, as follows:

1. Give great care to the selection, preliminary training, and installation of teachers.
2. Provide a capable assistant or associate teacher to be an understudy for each teacher on the faculty.
3. Thoroughly train all teachers and assistant teachers while they are in service.
4. Appoint all teachers for one year only, permitting a shifting of teachers when desired.

This "formula" cannot be put into practice quickly. Months and even years may be required to put them into practice. But a beginning can be made at any time, so *now* is the time to begin if your school has not done so already.

Here are some common problems. Let us see how the foregoing formula will help solve them.

The elderly, incompetent teacher. Often this teacher has a long record of faithful service and is loved by many. To hurt her feelings is unthinkable. How can you replace her? Two ways are suggested. A new class can be formed, made up of her long-time pupils; and she can be their teacher. Another teacher is chosen to teach the other pupils in the class. Or, if the plan for two classes is not practical, appoint an associate teacher, asking her to teach at least once a month. This associate teacher, being younger and more capable, will demonstrate to the class the need for better teaching; and in time, the elderly teacher can be named teacher-emeritus and be retired.

LOYAL WORKERS

The teacher who will not co-operate. A teacher's refusal to attend the regular conference of teachers and workers may indicate that the conference is not worth attending. It ought to be so attractive and vital in its appeal that every teacher and worker will attend. When a teacher is appointed, he or she ought to be instructed that attendance at the conferences is required as part of the training program. If a teacher does not attend, whether due to illness or absence from town or indifference, the departmental superintendent can call in the home and carefully go over all the details of the meeting. By the end of the year, when teacher appointments are to be made, the unco-operative teacher will either be co-operating, or will ask to be relieved of duty. Lack of co-operation can often be traced to lack of interest. Lack of interest is often due to lack of information. When a worker understands the necessity for an undertaking and is "sold" on it, he will usually co-operate to make it a success.

Habitual tardiness. This can be corrected by use of the Six-point Plan. (This will be discussed in chapter 14.) Teachers and workers are to be impressed by the fact that promptness is required. An alert superintendent will check the classrooms and assembly halls before the school opens to make sure that every worker is in place on time. When one is tardy, the defect must be called to the worker's attention, either by the departmental superintendent, if a teacher, or by the superintendent himself. Tardiness is a bad example to the pupils. It interferes with effective operation of the school.

The cigarette smoker. When a teacher is selected, he or she should put aside all questionable practices and habits, because actions speak louder than words. If this is not done, the teacher must be replaced at the annual selection of teachers.

The unprepared teacher. This teacher is one who usually puts off preparation until the last of the week, and then permits unexpected company or some other cause to interfere. Needless to say, such a teacher does not realize the importance of his position. He needs to be trained. At least once a year the workers' conference should give attention to "How I Prepare My Lesson."

Many other teacher problems could be listed. But these are enough to show you how the four-way formula will help you in solving them.

Do you know some of the many purposes of the workers' conference? They are listed for you on this page.

Who is supposed to attend the workers' conference? Why is the conference so important? These questions are answered on page 103.

Can you name the features that should be included in each workers' conference? Are you able to describe each feature? Pages 103 and 104 name and describe these features.

What are some of the topics that can be used for the educational feature of the workers' conference? Page 105 gives them for you.

Do you know how to promote attendance at the workers' conferences? Read page 105.

CHAPTER 13

YOU SUPERVISE

workers' conferences

"I would rather surrender my place as superintendent of a Sunday school than to be obliged to conduct it without a regular council or conference of my workers," said Marion Lawrance, famous Christian educator of a recent generation. Every superintendent should feel this way. No superintendent can hope to succeed without such a conference, held regularly and attended by all the school's workers.

WHAT IS A WORKERS' CONFERENCE?

A workers' conference is a meeting of the leading workers in the church's Sunday school, held at regular intervals. Each meeting offers opportunity for conference, training, fellowship, and inspiration. Here we have listed its purposes in their order of importance:

1. The workers' conference is a training session where workers learn the best ways to teach and perform the other tasks connected with the school.

2. It is a devotional fellowship, in which consecrated Christians with a common aim meet to consider the Lord's work to which they have been called.

3. It is an inspirational mountain peak where workers are encouraged and inspired to do better work.

4. It is a clinic for considering problems and finding their solutions.

5. It is a planning session in which progress is reviewed and plans are adopted for advancement.

6. It is a democratic meeting where each worker has a voice and a part.

7. The workers' conference brings the workers together under conditions that stimulate study, quicken interest, cement friendships, enlarge visions, deepen responsibility, and strengthen loyalty.

YOU SUPERVISE

Why is the workers' conference important? First of all, it offers part of the continuous training that every Sunday-school worker needs. Secondly, if the staff and faculty are to function as a team they need to confer regularly. In the third place, the programs of the church as a whole and of the school in particular need the support of every worker in the school. Lastly, the newly selected workers are made to feel that they are a part of the team when they attend the workers' conferences.

Who is to attend? Officers and teachers, assistant officers and teachers, the minister, members of the board of Christian education, and officers of the organized classes attend and participate equally. In some churches representatives of the youth groups, missionary society, and other educational organizations also attend. You, the superintendent, must make it definitely understood about who is to attend. A secretary should call the roll at each meeting, so that all will know who is participating.

When should the workers' conference meet? It should meet regularly, at the same hour and same day of the month, so that all members can reserve that time for the meeting. Usually the meetings are held monthly. Nothing else should be permitted to interfere with the time set for the conferences.

In some schools an executive committee, or steering committee, made up of the general superintendent and heads of departments, meets monthly; the general conference meets every two months. In other schools the meetings are held upon call. These plans do not utilize the most valuable benefit of the conference, which is the training session, but merely use it to inform members of plans and progress.

Where does it meet? The workers' conference may meet anywhere—in the church building, the homes of the members, the park for a picnic-meeting, etc. There is no set rule regarding the place. If it is a small school, social interest is heightened by holding the meetings in the homes of the members, where seasonal decorations may be employed and refreshments served. If the intention is to preserve a strictly businesslike atmosphere, however, the meeting should be held in one of the Sunday-school rooms. Some city schools hold the conference at a downtown place, such as the Y.M.C.A.

In any event, there should be an occasional social meeting such as a banquet at the beginning of the school year to welcome new members, a supper meeting, or picnic. A nursery should be provided to care for the small children of those who attend.

The Program. The usual workers' conference program in the average school follows this pattern:
1. Devotions—These include one or more hymns, Scripture reading, and prayer. A good plan is to have a different person each time to conduct this part of the program.
2. Reports—Minutes of the previous meeting, report of income and expenditures of the school, and departmental and activity reports are included.

WHERE TO MEET

SUNDAY-SCHOOL ROOM

HOME

PUBLIC BUILDING

3. Unfinished business—Reports on progress of activities planned at previous meetings are given.

4. New business—The workers take action on recommendations made by departments or committees, and plan for coming events.

5. Educational feature—This is the most important part of the program. It involves the much needed training for the workers.

6. Benediction—Close the session with a period of prayer.

7. Fellowship period—Refreshments are served, and the members visit with one another.

In larger schools, where the business is managed by the board of Christian education or by an executive committee, the workers' conference program is centered about a theme, without a transaction of business. In such cases the general session is followed by departmental meetings, in which each department reviews the theme as it applies to that particular department.

Departmental Conferences. Even in smaller schools it is profitable to hold departmental conferences, either before or after the general workers' conference. A popular plan is to hold the departmental conferences before a fellowship supper which precedes the general session. Thus the departments are enabled to bring reports and recommendations that are complete up to the time of the meeting.

In the better schools, the departmental groups meet weekly to discuss progress and solve problems. These meetings are sometimes held on Wednesday evening before or after the midweek service.

Weekly Workers' Conference. Some of the largest and fastest growing denominations encourage weekly meetings of all officers and teachers. Said one school, "It is much easier to have a good weekly meeting than an effective monthly meeting." The following schedule is popular:

6:00 to 6:30 P.M.—Fellowship supper.

6:30 to 6:45 P.M.—General promotion period, to discuss plans and progress, visitation, and other promotion of the school.

6:50 to 7:05—Departmental promotion, when department superintendents review the school's plans, as applied to the department, and assign definite work to the departmental staff. Past records are studied, visitation is planned, and departmental spirit is developed.

7:05 to 7:40—Teaching improvement periods, each department meeting separately under its own superintendent. In this meeting the workers discuss lesson preparation and presentation. Each one evaluates his own methods.

7:45 to 8:30—The church's midweek service, led by the minister.

Devotional Themes. The devotional period at each general conference should last between ten and fifteen minutes. Careful planning of the Scripture reading, hymns to be sung, and the purpose of the prayers is important. The themes may be seasonal.

Educational Features. This is the highly important part of every session. Here are some suggestions for possible topics:

How I Prepare My Lesson

How I Taught Last Sunday's Lesson

Evaluating the Lesson
Using Questions in Teaching
How to Make a Sunday-school Call
How to Use Flannelgraph
How to Use Object Lessons
Using a Map
Outlining the Lesson
Winning Pupils to Christ
How to Conduct a Successful Social
How to Create Interest in Missions

Increasing in popularity, also, is the use of educational filmstrips. Many are available, and the supply is growing. They cover such subjects as "The Growing Teacher," "The Laws of Sunday School Growth," "The Christian Teacher," "Selecting Aims," "Choosing the Best Teaching Method for Each Lesson," etc. Many of these filmstrips are audio-visual, with a record accompanying the filmstrip. All have manuals or guides for the leader's use. The best plan is to show the filmstrip once without comment, then to show it again, with discussion and comment on each picture. Such effective use of the usual filmstrip requires at least one hour.

HOW TO MAKE IT WORK

It is necessary to know not only what the workers' conference is and why it is important, but "how to make it work."

Promoting Attendance. A common complaint is, "Our workers do not attend our conferences." To avoid this complaint, follow these rules:

1. Expect the workers to attend. When an officer or teacher is selected, see that he understands that he is expected to attend every workers' conference.

2. Make the conferences worth attending. Books and periodical publications are available to help you plan your conferences.

3. Publicize the conference. A post card reminder of the time and place, with a "catchy" announcement of the feature attraction, is effective. Use the telephone also.

4. Call the roll at every meeting, noting absentees. Ask the departmental superintendents to call upon their absentee teachers and give them detailed reports of the meeting.

5. Begin and quit on time. Do not dawdle and waste precious minutes during the meeting.

6. Invite and urge participation. When a worker participates, even in brief fashion, he values the conference more than when he does not take part.

7. Emphasize the spiritual side. The Sunday school is part of the church and the church is the Lord's divinely provided agency for telling the world about Him. In a real sense Christ is an honored attendant at every conference. He is the head of the Sunday school.

Some Additional Ideas. At the beginning of the public-school year, invite the public-school superintendent or principal to tell how your Sunday school can help his school.

Invite the chief of police or a Christian judge to tell your officers and teachers how important their work is in solving juvenile delinquency and other crime.

Ask the superintendent, minister, or an exceptionally capable teacher from another church to lead in a discussion on some specific subject on which he or she is an authority.

The conference may enter upon a course of study, the book or books being studied at home and reviewed and discussed at the meeting.

Book reviews and the review of important articles pertaining to the Sunday school are good.

Round-table or panel discussions, "buzz" sessions, etc. on some particular subject are interesting diversions which may lead to new plans and ideas.

Introduce new members of the conference and ask them to say a few words.

The librarian can review new literature catalogs and new materials after which questions can be asked and answered.

If the church as a whole is undertaking some unusual project, ask the minister or committee chairman to tell about it and offer suggestions as to how the Sunday school can help.

Ask a teacher to bring her class of children to the conference for the purpose of demonstrating how she teaches a lesson.

As a group, visit a workers' conference in another church.

Hold an exhibit of training books, helpful publications, and teaching devices, with explanations.

The dramatization of a teacher counseling a pupil, a visit to an absentee or prospective member, or a personal talk with the minister about the Sunday school will be entertaining and instructive.

Occasionally a nationally known Sunday-school worker may be in the area and can be invited to appear before the conference to talk about his specialty and answer questions.

The Follow-Through. The superintendent's responsibility for the workers' conference does not end with the benediction. In a sense, it begins there. Plans approved by the conference are to be promoted to a successful conclusion. Committees are to be checked upon, to make sure they are doing their work properly. Participants in the conference are to be thanked for their help and congratulated upon their good work. The conference secretary is to make a carbon copy of the minutes of the meeting and give it to the superintendent within a day or two after the meeting, so that he can begin his important work of "following through."

What is the six-point plan? How can it help you, the superintendent, to supervise the pupils in your school? Read pages 107 and 108.

Why are organized classes valuable to your work of supervising? What four things can they do to help the Sunday school? These are listed for you on page 109.

Can you name five possible factors involved in discipline problems in the Sunday school? Pages 110 and 111 give you these factors.

Have you read pages 112 and 113? What should be done in the case of a "show-off" pupil? A habitually tardy person? The irregular attender? The "blocker"? The pupil who misbehaves? The chart on page 113 will also help you.

CHAPTER 14

YOU SUPERVISE

pupils

Who is the most important person in your school? The superintendent? The minister? The officer? The teacher? Every one of these is important—very important. But the MOST important person in your school is the pupil. The school exists for him. There would be no need for teachers, officers, and equipment were it not for the pupil. Christ died for him.

You are *indirectly* responsible for every pupil in your school. The teacher is *directly* responsible for the pupil; but you, as superintendent, must supervise. You must lead in helping the teacher solve such pupil problems as absenteeism, tardiness, lack of lesson preparation, non-attendance at the church's worship services, misbehavior, and failure to learn and apply in his daily living the great teachings of God's Word. How can you help to supervise the pupils in your school?

THE SIX-POINT PLAN

You need what is known as the "six-point plan." This is a simple plan which can easily be introduced into the school. It is a permanent method of improvement. As the name of the plan suggests, it has six purposes:

1. To encourage and to check the attendance of each pupil.
2. To encourage promptness and avoid tardiness.
3. To encourage giving.
4. To encourage each pupil to bring his own Bible.
5. To encourage lesson preparation.
6. To encourage attendance at the church's worship service.

Here is how the six-point plan works. On Sunday morning, as each pupil and teacher arrives, he is given a small envelope. On this

velope are spaces for him to write the date, his name, address, class and department. Several kinds of envelopes are available. The one pictured here is one kind.

Six spaces are shown in which each pupil and teacher is to check the six points and grade himself. He receives twenty points for being present, ten points for being on time, ten points for bringing his Bible, ten points for having an offering, thirty points for preparing his lesson in advance, twenty points for attending the church's worship service. There is then a space in which he writes his own grade. The goal is to have every member of the school make a grade of one-hundred points, or one-hundred per cent, every Sunday.

Below this row of check marks is a line on which each person is to note the number of personal calls and telephone calls he has made, and letters and cards he has sent during the week to invite absentees or new prospects to attend the Sunday school. Some schools use this line as the information for a "Boosters' Club." When a member makes five or more contacts during a week, he is a member of the club. The member of the school who makes the most contacts is the chief booster for the week in the entire school. Each class also may have its "Booster Club," with a chief booster each week.

The possibilities of this plan are immediately apparent. Properly promoted and used, it will bring about and maintain a high level of performance in the school.

As in any undertaking, proper promotion is necessary. To launch the plan, it is essential that every member of the school be carefully informed regarding it. Its benefits are to be pointed out and the school challenged to enter upon a program of improvement. First, you must "sell" the plan to the officers and teachers. Be sure they are informed in detail about the plan, the need for it, and the ways it will help the school. Enlist them to help "sell" the plan to the pupils. All the classes above the Primary Department, or third grade, can participate.

The six-point plan envelopes can be purchased from any publishing house or Bible bookstore at little cost.

The record keeping is not easy, but it must be done. Select capable persons for the work. The little envelopes will show the grade of each pupil. These can be added and divided by the number of pupils to learn the average in each class. These in turn can be added and divided by the total number of pupils in the Junior Department and above, to show the average for the school. The goal is for each pupil, class, and the entire school to attain one hundred per cent.

If the school or church publishes a weekly bulletin for distribution to the homes of the members, this bulletin can carry the names of those achieving one hundred per cent and the grades of the classes and of the school as a whole.

ORGANIZED CLASSES

Organized classes in the young people's and adult departments of your school can help you in your work of supervision. The organized class is valuable to your school for doing these four things:
1. Recruiting new members.
2. Maintaining regular attendance of enrolled members.
3. Helping to carry out the program of the school as a part of the church.
4. Training workers by giving them practice as class officers.

Suppose, for example, the church's general program calls for emphasis on stewardship. The school must help. The teachers will refer to the campaign and include instruction regarding it in their Sunday lessons. The organized classes will discuss it at their class meetings, usually held during the week. Perhaps class goals can be set, and the organized classes urged to strive to reach the goals.

The presidents, and sometimes all the officers, of these organized classes are invited to attend the workers' conferences. Thus they can lead their classes in co-operating closely in the program of the church and its school.

Many superintendents and other leading workers in the church gained their first experience by serving as class officers. A class secretary can develop into a school secretary. A class president can become an assistant superintendent of the school. The organized class aids in discovering and developing new workers.

The superintendent ought to keep in touch with the class organizations by attending some of the class meetings, conferring personally with newly-elected class officers, welcoming them at the workers' conference, and enlisting them in his program.

DISCIPLINE IS NO PROBLEM IF YOU KNOW HOW

"Problem pupils," like "problem teachers," will be brought to your attention. You will be asked, "What shall we do about it?" You must be able to get all the facts, analyze the situation, and recommend action.

Do not think that your problem of discipline is a new one. The cry of better discipline has been heard throughout the history of education. For almost three thousand years history has given us writings on discipline. You have no "problem pupil" who has not been duplicated thousands of times.

Remember that disorder breeds disorderliness. Do not blame the disorderly pupil for the disorderly school or class. It is the disorderly school or class that brings out the misbehavior of the pupil.

Keep the program moving. The devil still finds mischief for idle hands and minds. In the school, pass quickly from one part of the program to the next. See that the teachers do the same.

Poor discipline is often called the number one cause of teacher failure. Give the problem your best attention. Some common causes of poor discipline include the following:

1. *The teacher*. Nine out of ten "discipline" problems are teacher problems. A teacher who is irregular in attendance, often tardy, poorly prepared, untrained, who does not understand the needs of the pupils, lacks love for the Lord, His Bible, and the pupils, is the most frequent need for discipline, and the cause for problems. When there is a problem, first consider the teacher.

Every teacher of youngsters knows how pupils and classes "try him out" until he has set limits and they know what he will accept. Children want to admire and trust the teacher. They do not know it, but they want the security of a capable teacher who will keep them from hindering their own chances to learn. Thus, they try out the teacher to see if he is strong enough to be reliable.

The best of teachers is confronted with problem pupils. May it be said, however, that the trained and capable teacher can usually solve his own problems. One teacher of Junior boys was obliged to conduct her class in the church's kitchen because of overcrowded conditions. Nevertheless, her boys were noted for their orderliness and good behavior. She was a public-school teacher who loved boys of that age. She was trained and knew how to handle them. The first solution to any pupil problem, therefore, is to consider the teacher. He or she may need specific training in the psychology of the age group being taught.

2. *The pupil*. Every pupil is different. The home background, community environment, physical and mental handicaps must be taken into consideration. Sometimes the problem pupil comes from the home of a leader in the church. In any case, the pupil must be considered as an opportunity, not as a problem.

3. *The equipment*. Do the room and its furniture invite order or disorder? Uncomfortable, movable, and noisy chairs, benches on which pupils are crowded and therefore encouraged to "elbow" each other, poor lighting, uncomfortable temperatures, dust and dirt—all these are hazards and handicaps to good discipline.

4. *Curriculum.* Are the lessons interesting and within the pupils' understanding? Do they encourage pupil participation, hold his interest, promote an "I want to help" attitude on the part of the pupil? A good teacher can take poor curriculum material and adapt it to the pupils' interest. However, well-planned lessons, graded to the level of the child's understanding and true-to-the Bible, are essential materials for the average teacher in the Sunday school.

5. *Latecomers* often disturb and upset the orderly conduct of the class. Keep one or more vacant seating places near the entrance for these tardy ones. Perhaps the assistant teacher can act as usher, seeing that a minimum of disturbance is caused.

Disciplinary measures begin with good teaching, equipment, and curriculum. But sometimes even these fail. More help is needed. The basic principles of maintaining good discipline, in addition to those mentioned, are consistent firmness and kindness in dealing with the individual, impartiality toward pupils, and creation of a spirit of wanting to help because of the place and purpose.

The proper class spirit is important. The Lord's picture on the wall, an open Bible on the teacher's desk, the class session opened with a prayer inviting the Lord's presence and the Spirit to be in the heart of every pupil, and a reverent approach to the lesson will help discourage misbehavior. This is as true of the entire school as it is of a single class.

Sometimes, however, emergency measures are needed:

1. Little Sue or Johnny in the Kindergarten Department may continue to annoy after every possible way of reaching them as members of the group are exhausted. In such a case, she or he may be asked to take a book and sit in some designated place where close watch can be kept. The teacher must not appear to be disturbed and must not disrupt the class because of the incident. The little "problem" can be told that when she or he wants to join the class again they will be happy to have him.

2. An older child may be sent to the superintendent of the department or of the school and asked to explain why he is being sent. The superintendent will listen carefully to the child's side of the story, ask him for suggestions for improvement, and keep him in custody until the end of the lesson period. The teacher is to go to the child, tell him how sorry she is that he had to be punished, and invite him to cooperate. She must remember to hate the wrongdoing, but love the wrongdoer.

3. Ask the Lord's help. In public and private, pray for the pupils, that they may make the Lord happy by their behavior. Pray in private with an offending pupil.

4. Talk with the child's parents and public-school teachers, not as a tattler, but in a sincere, earnest attitude of asking for help.

Problem pupils in the early grades are easily handled. The teachers, some of whom are mothers, know how to deal with them. In the Junior,

Junior High, and Senior High classes, however, an individual pupil may be a chronic offender. Each is different from all the others in some ways, but there also are basic similarities. Let us see how the recommended disciplinary measures apply in some typical cases.

The show-off pupil. One teacher, about to resign because of such a pupil, was asked to pray for her fifteen minutes each day for two weeks before resigning. Her very first effort at prayer convinced her that she did not know enough about the girl to pray for her. She visited the pupil's home to get information. What she learned there led her to take particular interest in the child and to give her something to do in class that bestowed upon her the attention she craved. The girl responded with such promise that, years later, she became the teacher of the same class. The "show-off" type of pupil is usually hungry for attention. This hunger can be compensated by giving him or her some responsibility, such as reading the Scripture lessons or serving as the teacher's "right-hand man."

The habitually tardy pupil, if a child, may be the victim of circumstances beyond his control. His parents may lie in bed later than usual on Sunday. One teacher of Junior boys telephoned the homes of the habitually tardy pupils regularly every Sunday morning at an hour which would get them up early enough to be on time. The parents usually answered and the teacher asked to speak with the boy. If told he was still in bed, the teacher offered to telephone again in a few minutes. When the boy answered, the teacher urged him to be present at Sunday school on time. Emphasis on the six-point plan also helps encourage promptness. Another device is to give some little award to pupils who are present on time for a certain period. Still another is to use one of the attendance wall charts which provides the pupil's attendance record and shows whether or not he was on time. If the pupil's parents attend, the teacher may co-operate with the officers of the parents' class in getting them there on time. If the parents do not attend, the best solution to the problem is to get them to enroll and attend regularly.

Irregular attendance will be discussed later in detail. If a child is frequently absent because the parents, who do not attend, take him on Sunday trips, the best solution is to enlist the parents.

The "blocker" or argumentative pupil who wants to debate every point and oppose every suggestion is a common problem. A person, whether child or grown-up, who experiences nothing but frustration and defeat in his relationship with people will nurse this negative attitude as a defense mechanism. Expert teachers will use praise whenever possible in dealing with this type, ignoring the stubborn attitudes. Such a pupil needs to have a feeling that he is wanted by the group. Once he has a sense of security, he can become an asset to the class.

The misbehaving pupil often can be guided aright. A teacher arrived in the classroom to find the chalkboard decorated with chalk cartoons. He quietly erased the cartoons and began the lesson. Fully aware of the identity of the cartoonist, he asked him later if he had

YOU SUPERVISE

drawn the cartoons. The pupil reluctantly acknowledged his work. The teacher then said that he had been looking for someone who could help him with the chalkboard work during the lesson. The boy agreed to help and faithfully outlined the lesson on the chalkboard each week. All that a teacher needs to do is to demonstrate his confidence in himself and in his pupils. A capable teacher takes hold of any troublesome situation and builds on it so that in the end something good develops. Remember, no pupil is ever a "problem," he is an "opportunity."

The following chart, taken from the book *Teach With Success*, copyrighted 1956 by The Standard Publishing Foundation and used here by permission, lists various behavior problems and suggests corrective action.

SUGGESTED CORRECTIVE ACTION FOR BEHAVIOR PROBLEMS

When the Pupil Acts Like This ➤ ➤ Here's What You Can Do

	Pray for Him	Give Lesson Assignment	Set a Good Example	Frequently Cite Good Examples	Offer a Reward for Good Achievement	Have a Personal Talk With Pupil	Give the Pupil Special Attention	Let Pupil Know What Is Expected of Him	Make Lessons More Interesting	Ask a Good Pupil to Be His "Buddy"	Investigate Background	Give Pupil More Responsibility	Introduce a Class Project
Attends Irregularly	x		x		x	x			x				
Fails to Pay Attention	x	x				x		x			x		x
Learns Slowly	x	x				x	x	x					x
Seems Overly Timid	x				x	x				x	x		
Likes to "Show Off"	x	x									x	x	
Appears to Be Antagonistic	x	x	x								x		x
Tries to Domineer	x							x			x	x	
Is Always Tardy	x		x			x	x				x		
Lacks Reverence	x		x	x		x					x		
Does Not Attend Church Services	x		x	x	x	x		x			x		
Does Not Prepare Lesson	x	x	x		x				x				x
Brings No Offering	x		x					x					x
Seems Overly Aggressive	x			x							x	x	

Encourage the workers in your school to come to you with their problems. If it is a teacher, be sure that the departmental superintendent is included in the effort to find the right solution. If it is an officer, you can help him or go with him to someone who can be of help, such as the minister, chairman of the board of Christian education, or another worker in the school.

Also encourage teachers to discuss their problems with public-school teachers who work in the corresponding grades. The public-school men and women are trained and experienced. They also are more often than not eager to help in Christian work and are sincerely interested in their age groups.

As superintendent, you must listen patiently and do your best to help your fellow-workers to clear up their grievances. But where they are able to solve their own problems, urge them to do so.

Here is a check list to help you decide what you do or do not do to promote good discipline in your school. As you read the ten items, circle either the 1, 2, or 3 after each statement. Circling 1 means that the statement reflects your usual practice or attitude; circling 2 means it is not your frequent practice or attitude; circling 3 means that you are opposed to the practice or attitude.

I show immediate and warm interest in the problems brought to me by the members of my school.	1	2	3
I try to find the strong points of every worker and urge him to find something of value in each pupil.	1	2	3
I stimulate workers to learn to solve their own problems and at the same time make them feel free to come to me.	1	2	3
I do not irritate everyone with regulations designed to control only a few offenders.	1	2	3
I refrain from the use of sarcasm, discourteous remarks, or offensive humor in dealing with others.	1	2	3
I avoid throwing cold water on the suggestions of others with such comments as "We've always done it this way."	1	2	3
I make needed decisions tactfully and fairly, but promptly and finally.	1	2	3
I am conscientious about keeping promises made to an individual, my fellow workers, or to the school.	1	2	3
Realizing that conditions change, I readily accept necessary changes in methods and regulations.	1	2	3
I am careful to set the right example by my habits, practices, conduct, and behavior.	1	2	3

Can you name the seven rules for building good attendance in the Sunday school? Can you describe each rule? Read pages 115 through 118.

What is the best method for publicizing or promoting the church and Sunday school? Why? Read page 119 for the answers to these questions.

What four "P's" are required for recruiting new members for the Sunday school and church? Page 119 lists them for you.

Can you describe two plans for recruiting new pupils? Page 120 will help you.

What three factors are involved in rescuing absentees? Can you tell why each is important? After you read page 121 you will be able to answer these questions.

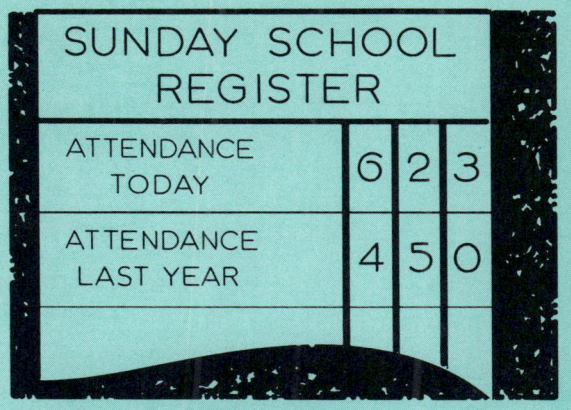

CHAPTER 15

YOU SUPERVISE

attendance

SEVEN RULES FOR BUILDING ATTENDANCE

The Sunday school has two basic attendance jobs:

1. To recruit for Christ (enrolling new pupils and leading them to become Christians).

2. To conserve for Christ (helping the recruits to grow as Christians and to remain faithful).

Methods of accomplishing these purposes in the Sunday school may differ somewhat in details, but basically they are the same. They conform to what can be called the "seven rules for building attendance." Let us list these seven rules, discuss each briefly, then consider some detailed methods.

1. The rule of the PROPER INCENTIVE.
2. The rule of SPECIFIC OBJECTIVES.
3. The rule of ADEQUATE FACILITIES.
4. The rule of a CONSECRATED STAFF.
5. The rule of the RIGHT CURRICULUM.
6. The rule of a PREPARED PROGRAM.
7. The rule of PUBLICITY.

1. *Proper Incentive.* Why do you want to increase the attendance in your school? If you take a pencil and write down some answers they will probably be these: The Lord commanded it, and we must obey Him; Christian concern for others compels us to increase the attendance. If we take the Sunday-school enrollment figures and com-

pare them with the United States census reports, we find that two out of three children up to twelve years old, three out of four young people up to twenty-four years old, and six out of seven adults over twenty-five are not receiving a Christian education of any kind. They are growing up as pagans in a so-called Christian land! Millions of people die every year without the promise of eternal life.

This love of the Lord and concern for others provide the incentive for enlisting new pupils. It also compels us to be concerned about those on the Sunday-school roll. In his *Sunday School Handbook* (copyright 1939 by The Standard Publishing Company and quoted here by special permission), James DeForest Murch tells of a little boy who quit attending his class in a large church to go to a mission Sunday school. When he was asked why, he said, "They love a fellow down there."

2. *Specific Objectives*. To get anywhere you have to know where you are going. A Sunday school, therefore, ought to have a goal. That goal is to reach for Christ every unreached person in the school's area. The best way to achieve that goal is to take a census to learn who is unreached, then conduct a campaign to bring them into the school.

Another plan is to enlist the school in a continuous program of step-by-step growth. For example, if the average attendance is one hundred per Sunday, a goal of 110 per Sunday can be set for the next month, 120 for the next, and so on. Such goals can be broken down and portioned out to the departments and classes. In other words, every class, department, and the entire school should have a specific goal for every Sunday in the year.

To achieve the goals of their school and classes, individuals must be encouraged to participate. The church is a group activity. Those in the church grow spiritually as they work wholeheartedly in purposeful activity. Enlisting others is such an activity.

The Sunday school is not like the public school, or factory, or other places where attendance is required by law or economic necessity. Attendance is voluntary. Those who attend must come because they want to come, and those who bring them must be encouraged to win others. This encouragement is given by recognition, which may be an award of some kind, etc.

Group participation can be encouraged also by friendly rivalry, commonly called a contest. When the members of a Sunday school are encouraged to look upon themselves as human beings performing necessary roles to achieve purposeful goals in the spirit of Christian love and zeal, then the group begins to be spiritually productive. It is not merely going through routine and therefore monotonous activities; it is moving forward toward a specific objective or goal.

3. *Adequate Facilities*. An attractive, well-equipped place for every pupil, teacher, and officer is desirable, but not immediately necessary. Such facilities should be the school's aim. The public schools, in these days of robust juvenile population growth, have taught that everyone can be accommodated, even though it is with temporary facilities.

Sunday schools long have known that they can grow, even with inadequate facilities. One bustling and rapidly growing Sunday school in St. Petersburg, Florida, called its Juniors the "carport department," because the Junior classes met temporarily in residential carports along the streets. A large Texas school housed its rapidly growing Primary Department in a public school building six blocks from the church building. The pupils paraded each Sunday from their classrooms to the church building for their worship program. An Oklahoma church boasted of a young married people's class that met in a nearby mortuary. Almost every church can tell of using emergency facilities. No one will claim these are better than a well-equipped classroom in a building erected for educational purposes, but all will agree that no Sunday school has to claim inadequate facilities as an excuse for not trying to grow.

4. *Consecrated staff.* In a previous chapter we mentioned the "law of ten": divide the attendance of the Sunday school by ten and usually the result will be the number of officers and teachers in the school. For each worker, according to the "law of ten," there are ten pupils. This means that the growing Sunday school has as many officers and teachers as it possibly can use. The more officers and teachers it has, the more pupils and the greater attendance there are.

Another "law" is divide and multiply. It is based on the tried and proved fact that the more classes a Sunday school has, the larger is its attendance. No classes are ever combined in a growing school, but at every opportunity a class is divided. Soon each of the two classes will equal in attendance the average attendance of what was formerly one class, doubling the attendance. A newly-formed class grows faster than an old one. Its growth is an encouragement to the entire school. The same is true of departments. Just as soon as the Kindergarten Department, for instance, can be divided, the division is made and there are two Kindergarten Departments. Each of them will soon be developed to equal the attendance of the former one department.

What do these two "laws" mean? They mean that consecrated, conscientious workers are needed—more and more of them.

They also mean that a school should be graded, with a separate class for every age group.

Perhaps most important of all, this rule of the consecrated staff means that every officer and teacher in the school is studying and working to do the best job possible. Nothing builds attendance like an interesting, engaging lesson, during which the pupil learns. Without a consecrated staff all other attendance effort is wasted.

5. *Right Curriculum.* This rule means that the Bible is taught, and that its teachings are applied to the daily life of each pupil. We no longer ask whether a curriculum is "Bible centered," or "pupil centered," or "experience centered," or "social," or "evangelistic." It ought to be all these—and more. Merely to teach Bible facts is not enough.

Some schools overdo the factual teaching and some overdo the application. It is not enough to say that all the pupil must know is what the Bible teaches and he will apply the teaching to his own life. The devil knows the Bible by heart, but has certainly not applied its teachings to himself.

Nor is the application of the Bible teaching enough. In one Sunday-school class of Juniors the teacher, laboring over literature that had been given her, talked at length about the migrant problem in the United States. Asked later if she taught the Bible, she exclaimed, "Oh, I forgot to tell the Bible story!"

The rule of the right curriculum also means that the Bible is to be taught as a divine textbook, infallible, complete, and authoritative. It should be presented as the inspired Word of God.

The right curriculum is also a graded curriculum, written especially for the understanding of each pupil, with special teaching helps for the teacher.

6. *Prepared Program*. To grow, a Sunday school must follow a prepared program. This may be a program of advancement outlined by the local church, or some published plan for achievement. Included in such a program should be plans for increasing attendance, training leaders, obtaining better equipment, organizing effectively, bringing about decisions for Christ, and perhaps witnessing in the home, the community, and the world.

Such a program also provides a time schedule, perhaps with seasonal, monthly, and weekly objectives. A properly supervised school will know what is planned for at least one year in advance.

The law of the prepared program applies also to Sunday morning. A school that follows a dull routine and proceeds in haphazard fashion is not likely to grow. A school that functions smoothly, with carefully planned and varied programs is a winner.

7. *Publicity*. A better word is "promotion," but is often confused with "Promotion Day." Hence, the word "publicity" is used.

Another good word would be "salesmanship." The rule of publicity means that the Sunday-school program is sold to the workers, pupils, homes, and community. The usual methods of using the newspaper and radio, sending cards and letters through the mail, advertising on billboards and with posters, and calling people on the telephone are all good ways to publicize the Sunday school and church. Much could be said about the use of each of these in building Sunday-school attendance. If possible, the Sunday school should have a chairman of publicity who will see to it that the school's plans and accomplishments are given the widest possible publicity.

The best method of all, however, is personal visitation, or the ringing of doorbells and the invitation to attend the school extended in person to relatives, friends, and neighbors. No method of publicity equals that of word of mouth. When Mrs. Washday greets her neighbor, Mrs. Monday, over the backyard fence and tells her neighbor that her washing is always so clean and bright because she uses such-and-such a soap, that is the best advertising there is. Any business firm prizes such advertising above all other kinds. In like manner, when Mr., Mrs., and Miss Sunday School recommend the church to another, that is the best church advertising there is.

The largest, fastest growing Sunday schools in America maintain a vigorous program of visitation. Officers, teachers, and other workers are given a list of calls to make every week. They meet during the week to make their reports. Lists of prospective members are obtained by a community census, or from relatives, friends, or neighbors. The prospective members are called upon and invited to attend the school. Careful records are kept of the calls and every call is followed up. Such a program of visitation requires training, time, and effort. But it pays as no other work of enlistment will pay.

Another method is to enlist every pupil, officer, and teacher in the Sunday school, including every member of the church, and if possible, every person in the community in the work of building attendance. Little Master Beginner, from his first day in the Kindergarten Department, can help by inviting others. Everyone can help. First, however, the church must become "Sunday-school minded." It must realize the importance of the Sunday school, the importance of increasing attendance, and the fact that the Sunday school is the church at work recruiting and conserving for Christ before it will grow as it should. Leading the church to take this view of its Sunday school is up to the superintendent.

METHODS OF RECRUITING

To recruit new members, these four "P's" are required:

P-ROSPECTS: These are found by a community census, or by asking pupils for names of relatives and friends who do not attend.

P-ROPERTY, or classroom space. But do not delay action just because you do not have perfect facilities.

P-ERSONNEL, or officers and teachers, consecrated and trained, or in training.

P-UBLICITY, which means "Go out, tell people, and bring them in."

Some churches are so dignified that they do not encourage members to invite the unreached to attend Sunday school. They fear that to do more than open the doors and ring the bell on Sunday morning will lower the church in public esteem. They forget two things:

1. Christianity is an emergency appeal. People are dying without Christ. We dare not stand idly by. When a neighbor's house catches on fire and the family is asleep inside we do not put on our best visiting attire, stroll calmly up the walk and gently ring the bell! We bang on the door and yell! In like manner, we must help the sinner

to realize that he is in terrible danger. The least we can do is invite and urge him to attend Sunday school.

2. The church of the New Testament did not stand on dignity. Read the first four verses of the second chapter of Acts. "Suddenly there came a sound from heaven as of a rushing mighty wind . . . and [they] began to speak with other tongues." No wonder the "multitude came together, and were confounded" (verse 6). Jesus performed miracles, denounced evil with the most forceful language ever uttered on this earth, and cleansed the temple with a whip. The church's work is to be done decently and in order according to the Scriptures, but it is not to be smothered in a pious pillow of dignity. Common sense must rule. Do not be afraid to resort to proper promotional efforts to build attendance in the Sunday school.

Following are typical plans which have worked and are working in Sunday schools to encourage the recruiting of new pupils.

The Fishermen's League. This plan is based on Mark 1:17: "And Jesus said unto them, Come ye after me, and I will make you to become fishers of men." When a new member is brought to the school and has attended three Sundays, the one who brings him is recognized by having his name placed on a "Fishermen's League" poster. This poster may be kept on display in the classroom or school auditorium where everyone can see it. A colored star is added for each additional member that the "fisherman" brings. At some designated time each year, special recognition is given to all "fishermen."

The Two-by-Two Plan. Personal calling is the best way to enlist new pupils. In Mark 6:7 we read that Jesus "called unto him the twelve, and began to send them forth by two and two." In a two-by-two campaign, the callers meet at the church, sometimes for a sack lunch, and after a brief devotional service receive the names of the prospects upon whom they are to call. They make the calls, then return to the church and report.

An interesting adventure to add to this plan is for each couple to make one "blind" call—that is, to call at some house along the route without that call having been designated. The couple will interview the people who live in the house and bring back a report of their experiences and findings.

New Member Committee. Since there are two parts to the program of building attendance, a school, class, or department may be divided into two parts with a director or "captain" over each. One group has as its particular function the enlistment of new members. The other group is responsible for bringing back absentees. The first group is responsible for each prospective member until he has attended three times and is enrolled. From then on the second group takes over.

Other plans have been employed successfully to enroll new pupils in the school. None, however, has succeeded without work. Plan your work of enlistment, then work your plan vigorously and persistently, and you will succeed.

RESCUE THAT ABSENTEE!

A study of Sunday-school attendance showed that only about half of those enrolled in Sunday school are present on an average Sunday. The actual figures were these:
Enrollment—7,112,411
Average Attendance (in 38,350 Sunday schools)—3,685,220

An even more alarming observation is that seven out of ten adults who do not attend Sunday school were at one time regular in attendance. Such desertion, or backsliding, usually occurs between the ages of twelve and fifteen. It is directly traceable to the fact that the parents do not attend. The solution to this problem is to enlist the parents in active attendance.

At all ages, however, absenteeism is a problem. Pupils are permitted to fall away, often with little or no effort to rescue them. Notice we use the word "rescue." It is pictured in the Lord's parable of the lost sheep. Special effort is necessary to rescue the absentee. This effort involves three factors.

1. *Records.* When a pupil is absent, immediate action is necessary. This requires a secretarial system that records and reports the attendance of each pupil. This is usually done in each class. The assistant teacher may make the record in children's classes; classes of older pupils may have their own secretaries. This record may be a class book, card index, etc.

2. *Notification.* When a pupil is absent, the responsible party is immediately notified. This may be the teacher or assistant teacher, or the attendance officer in a class of adults. As quickly as possible, the absentee is to be contacted. Usually a telephone call is adequate to learn whether the pupil is ill. A personal "just dropped in to ask" call is best. At the least a card can be sent to the absentee saying, "We missed you."

3. *Method of Rescue.* So serious is an absence that a complete program of follow-up is necessary. Most cases of absence can be disposed of by merely notifying the one who is responsible for starting the rescue, and then this person's notifying the absentee that he was missed. A second absence without adequate reason calls for more serious action. A personal call must be made to learn the member's reason for absence and to urge his return. This call is the responsibility of the teacher or, if in an older class, the attendance officer. A third absence may require a visit by the superintendent or minister. In every case, the pupil is to be convinced that he is missed, that his return is important to his spiritual welfare, and that the very next Sunday is the best time to return.

Seldom does an absentee fail to return when he is approached as described. Should he remain among the backsliders, however, he is not to be forgotten. He is to be invited to all school activities, called upon when visitation is made for special days, and is to receive attention as a likely prospect for future regular attendance.

METHODS OF CONSERVATION

The foregoing plan of checking, following up, and bringing back the absentee is good. But it is even better to *prevent* absenteeism. This can be done by following the seven rules for building attendance. Special means may be employed, however, to encourage faithfulness.

The Honor Roll. Place the names of all members of the school or class on an Honor Roll. The name of each person stays on the roll as long as he attends without missing. When he is absent, his name is removed or covered in some way, and he must attend three consecutive Sundays before his name can be restored on the roll. A picnic or other special recognition for those whose names are on the Honor Roll more than six months of the year will be an added incentive. Any absenteeism results in a removed name except attendance at another Sunday school.

52 Club. On the first Sunday of the year, or on any Sunday of the year, announce that all who are present are being honored by receiving membership in the "52 Club." Distribute "52 Club" pins, which are available at any religious book store or publishing house at low cost. Each person is a member in good standing and may wear his club pin proudly until he is absent. One absence eliminates him as a "52 Club" member for the current year. On the last Sunday of each month have a "52 Club" roll call by asking those to stand who have perfect attendance records since the beginning of the club.

In this case, as with the Honor Roll, any absence, unless the member is attending another Sunday school, breaks the record. This rule is necessary to avoid confusion over excuses for absence.

Charts and Cards. Wall charts, individual award cards, and similar devices for promoting uninterrupted attendance, particularly by children, are available in beautiful designs and large variety. They have long proved to be an excellent means by which faithful and regular attendance can be encouraged.

Award Pins. Several attractive plans for award pins are available. In each case, every pupil receives a pin. As his record of unbroken attendance lengthens, he receives more expensive pins with wreaths, bars, or numbered disks to be added. Before such a program of awards is undertaken it is well to consider the expense involved. A Sunday school cannot afford to start a plan of awards and then fail to live up to its promises.

To repeat, however, any system for following up absentees and giving awards to the faithful must be supported by good teaching, good equipment, and a good school. Pupils cannot be expected to continue coming unless these incentives make attendance worthwhile.

How can a one-room church building be prepared so that several classes can meet satisfactorily? Page 125 discusses this problem.

Why are proper lighting, ventilation, and room temperature important in the Sunday-school classroom? What can be done to insure having these things? Read page 126.

Can you name some of the furnishings that each classroom should have? Why is each type of furnishing important? You can find out by reading page 127.

Why is it important to select the "right" person to be custodian of Sunday-school equipment? What are some of his duties? How can he help the teachers and other workers to make the best use of the equipment? Read page 130.

CHAPTER 16

YOU SUPERVISE

equipment

On the way home from church one Sunday morning a little girl asked her mother, "Mommy, is God poor?"

Surprised by such a question, the mother quickly replied, "Why no, darling. God is rich. He owns everything."

The child thought a moment, then said, "The church is God's house, isn't it?"

"Yes," answered the puzzled parent. "Why do you ask?"

"Well, if He is rich, why does He have dirty old furniture in my Sunday-school classroom? We have nicer things in our house than He has in His!"

What impression does your school's equipment make? Impressions are important. The little girl was being taught *by the classroom furnishings* to disbelieve in God! The teacher was teaching one thing; the furnishings were teaching another.

Take a look at your Sunday-school building, the classrooms, the furnishings. What do they teach? And while we are considering equipment, let us take a look also at the classroom materials and stockroom of teaching equipment and supplies.

A LOOK AT THE BUILDING

If your church does not have a Sunday-school building, usually called the educational plant, you probably are planning one. So important does the church consider its school that such an educational

plant is often erected before there is an auditorium for the worshipers. This has become perhaps the most significant change in church building in the present century. In the early 1900's, few churches had special buildings for their Sunday schools. Today, almost every church has such a special building or plans to build one.

For such buildings careful planning is necessary. Usually there is a "Master Plan" for the church property as a whole. The Sunday-school building is part of that plan. It may be a separate structure or it may be part of the one main church building. It may even be several buildings.

A Florida church, starting in a new location, first built a chapel for the worship service, using as its Sunday-school building a large residence already on the property. Next it erected a building for the adult classes, so arranged that it could also be used for a social hall. Then a building for the Young People's Department was built, followed by one for the Juniors, another for the Primary, another for the Preschool and Nursery Departments, and finally, the main worship auditorium. The buildings, in a half-circle, were connected by a walk and overhead porch roof that continued all the way around. The yard within the half-circle was beautifully landscaped for use for outdoor services. In the rear of the half-circle was the parking area.

How different this was from the arrangement in another church, where the Sunday-school plant was constructed at considerable cost in the basement of a new worship structure. A narrow hallway along the middle of the basement was flanked on either side by small, narrow classrooms, each with a small window near the ceiling, and each walled in by brick walls. "It's for all the world like a jail!" exclaimed a visiting Sunday-school worker, who urged that the brick walls between the rooms be removed and movable cabinets or screens be used to divide the classes.

These "good" and "horrible" examples are offered merely to emphasize that careful planning, by someone who knows what is needed, must be employed in building for a Sunday school. Few situations are the same. Each needs individual attention. There are books of plans and suggestions that can be studied. A builder or architect may mean well, but unless he knows what is needed in a good Sunday-school building, he is likely to draw up impractical plans.

For example, the school is departmentalized; and the building ought to be constructed for departments rather than for single, separate classes. The reasons for this are obvious. One is that the departments hold their own one-hour services each Sunday morning, without meeting with the others for an opening or closing. To do this, the departmental section ought to be constructed to permit flexibility in arrangement.

Larger educational buildings provide an assembly room for each department with classrooms opening into it, or a separate building for each department, the classes being divided by folding partitions, cabinets, or screens. These are described in detail in the many books on this subject.

"But what about the one-room church building?" is a good question. There are books about the small, one-room church building too. If yours is such a building, you ought to make use of these books. They contain many suggestions. One is that small children be seated on low benches and use the seat of a pew for a table. Another is that metal rings be attached to pews so that light metal rods can be inserted in a moment's time to support simple screens of plain cloth that will divide the auditorium into classrooms.

Care must be taken, whether the school has its own building or is in the auditorium of a one-room church building, to allow for quick escape in the event of fire or other emergency. Strict laws require this in most places.

Good air-conditioning and lighting also are demanded in this age of improvement. Correct temperature at all times is necessary in a successful school. As for the lighting, ask the electric utility company to send one of its counselors, whose services are free, to go over the school with you and offer suggestions for improvement.

The colors used in painting the walls and ceilings are important also. Scientific studies have been made; and the information is available at paint stores, telling how people react to different colors. Visit the public schools and note the colors used there.

Cleanliness is important. Clean walls, ceilings, and floors, clean furniture and draperies must be the rule. Remember the story of the little girl who asked, "Is God poor?"

The day is here when church buildings are planned for increasing activities. It is not sensible, economical, or Christian to build at a high cost, then permit the building to lie idle except for a brief period on Sunday morning. Maximum use of space is now recommended. An increasing number of churches are conducting duplicate services; the younger pupils studying while the older pupils worship, and the older ones studying while the younger pupils worship. Some churches have a number of Sunday morning, afternoon, and evening classes and worship groups, with many church activities during the week. You are basically responsible for the Sunday-morning hour, but you and your fellow Sunday-school workers are interested in the whole program of the church. You will want to see that the property is used and cared for properly while it is under your jurisdiction.

A PEEK INTO THE CLASSROOMS

Whether yours is a small building or an educational plant with multiple departmentalization, there are standard classroom requirements which your school should strive to meet. I say "strive to meet" because these requirements are for the ideal school. Not many schools come up to the ideal at present. But every school can keep the following recommendations in mind and try to achieve them. No school can become the "ideal" school all at once.

Good housekeeping is one ideal to strive for. Neatness and cleanliness are possible anywhere. Attractiveness is another goal. Every classroom ought to be as attractive as possible. Encourage your departmental workers and faculty in this effort. Praise the attractive classroom. Take your workers to visit Sunday schools that have such classrooms.

Sensible arrangement is another goal. A class of adults, wondering why their enrollment did not increase, investigated and realized that the pupils were so seated that they faced a bright window. The Sunday-morning sun hurt their eyes. Arrange the classroom so that the lighting is helpful, not offensive. Put the teacher in the back of the room with her back to the wall, so that latecomers will not have to parade in front of her while teaching. The seating should permit pupils to find seats without having to "climb over one another." In a one-room building where the classes met in the auditorium without screens to give them privacy, the teachers stood against the wall, on the side away from the aisle, so that pupils' eyes were not distracted.

Sensible arrangement sometimes calls for rearrangement of classes. The tiny tots and the oldest people, for example, should not have to climb stairs. The assignment of classes to rooms is the responsibility of the board of Christian education. The superintendent should not take this responsibility upon himself.

Adequate space is a frequent problem in these times of the fast-growing Sunday school, and it is important. The required space for each pupil varies with the age of the pupil. The active child of preschool age, unaccustomed to schoolroom confinement, and full of energy, requires the most space; the adults require the least. Crowding interferes with learning. On the other hand, too much space per pupil is objectionable. A comfortable situation, with no crowding and with no lonely, discouraging, empty chairs, is best. Page 127 gives the amount of space that each class should have.

Proper lighting requires attention. Glaring light is as objectionable as too little light. Curtains can be used to regulate the light from outside windows. The specialist from the electric light company can advise you.

Proper ventilation is important. Stuffy air makes sleepy minds. An electric fan blowing into the face of a pupil keeps him from learning, just as does a hot ray of sun shining upon him through a window.

Maintaining proper room temperature requires that the room be kept warm enough in the cool months and cool enough in the warm months. Air conditioning is rapidly becoming the solution in many parts of the country. Complete comfort may not always be possible, but usually something can be done to help an undesirable situation.

FURNISHINGS ARE IMPORTANT

Chairs and tables, like the lesson, should be graded to fit the pupil's needs. This equipment is discussed further on page 127 in connection with the needs of each department.

Clothes hangers and racks are to be provided so that wraps will not be draped over chairs and pews. These, like the chairs, tables, and Bible lessons are graded. Little Susie, five years old, hangs up her own hat and coat on a clothes rack suited to her height. She may even have an animal, bird, or flower to show which coat hanger is hers. These clothes racks and hangers should be separate furniture which can be moved from room to room if necessary.

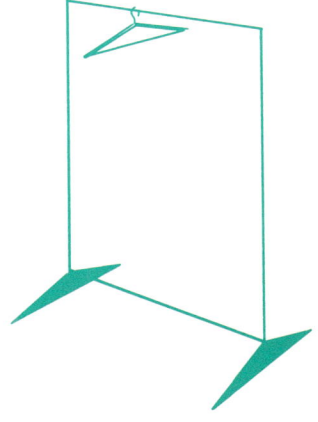

A supply cupboard is a "must" in every room. It is needed for storing the handwork, papers, quarterlies, erasers, chalk, and other items needed by the teacher. These supplies are valuable, and ought to be protected. Because the closely-graded lessons are usually the same each year for several years, the teachers' manuals, unused pupils' materials, pictures, and other teaching supplies can be kept and used again and again at a considerable saving. In almost every church there are carpenters and cabinet makers who can build the necessary cupboards. Overhanging cupboards may be used to conserve floor space. Or, cupboards may be built with coasters, so they can be rolled in and out of the classrooms as they are needed.

Chalkboards, tackboards, and other permanent equipment may be attached to the walls. Modern educational buildings have them installed in the walls. Flannelboards, projection screens, a place for maps, and television screens may be similarly installed. In older buildings these things can be portable and kept in a central storeroom for the use of the teachers.

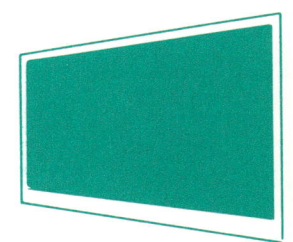

In addition to the foregoing needs of all classrooms, each grade has its own special requirements. These differ with the grades as follows:

NURSERY:

The classroom should contain twelve to fifteen pupils, with twenty-five to thirty square feet per pupil. The legal standard for public nurseries is forty square feet. It ought to be on the ground floor, having southern exposure, with many windows, floored with linoleum, covered with a rug. In some nurseries a germ-destroying type of light is used for sanitation.

The furnishings include chairs up to ten inches in height, with square or round tables not higher than ten inches above the seats of the chairs. Pictures are to be at the eye level of the pupil.

Teaching materials, in addition to the usual pictures and toys, could be a piano, record player and an unbreakable receptacle for receiving the offering.

BEGINNER:

The classroom should be on the ground floor, contain ten to twelve pupils, allowing twenty-five to thirty square feet per pupil. Clear glass windows, low enough for the pupils to see out, will add to their feeling of security. A linoleum or cork floor with rugs on which the children sit for floor stories, pictures at eye level for the children, and cheerful, homelike decorating are good.

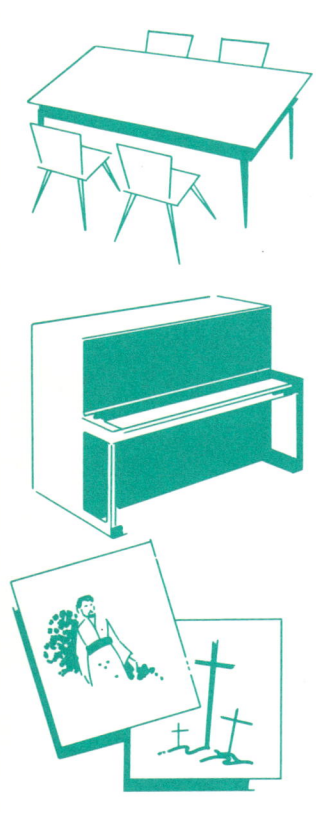

The furnishings are to be low, round tables, ten inches from the seat of the chairs; low chairs, ten to twelve inches high; teacher's desk, piano, record player, small table for flowers, comfortable chairs for visitors, and a wastebasket.

Teaching materials for the Beginners' room include, in addition to the usual quarterlies: pictures, handwork, activity books, blunt scissors, crayons for coloring, clay, paper, paste and unbreakable receptacle for the offering, a sand table and accompanying toys.

PRIMARY:

The classroom can be a section of a larger room, shut off by curtains or screens, with the usual chalkboard and other permanent fixtures. These children attend public school, therefore the room may partake of the nature of a schoolroom, with twenty-five square feet per pupil, with ten to twelve pupils in each class.

The furnishings are the chairs, fifteen inches high; the table, ten inches above the seat of the chair; piano; pictures at the pupils' eye level; and the ever-necessary cabinet.

Teaching materials for the Primaries are many: the usual workbooks, activity sets, handwork, Bible and quarterly for the teacher; and such special things as wastebaskets, colored construction paper, scissors, crayons and pencils, songbooks, the offering receptacle and, for this age for the first time—maps. Sand trays and toys will help.

JUNIOR:

The classroom is another schoolroom, and partitions instead of screens and curtains are more necessary than in the Primary Department. The Junior group should include not more than twenty to twenty-five, with twenty-five to thirty square feet per pupil rated as good; twenty to twenty-five as fair; and under twenty square feet, poor.

The furnishings are less numerous than for the younger grades, but include chairs fourteen to sixteen inches high and a table ten inches above the seat of the chairs. Rubber-tipped chair legs will lessen noise. The picture screen and bulletin boards must still be kept at the pupils' eye level.

Teaching materials now feature the Bible, one for each pupil, in addition to the workbooks, activity kits, pictures, handwork equipment, wastebasket, offering receptacle, and—for this age—a relief map of the area being studied.

JUNIOR HIGH or INTERMEDIATE:

The classroom is now definitely a schoolroom, partitioned off from other classes if possible. Curtains or screens can be used better than with Juniors. With twenty in the class, fifteen to twenty square feet per pupil is good; twelve to fifteen, fair; under twelve feet, poor. The chalkboard is a permanent fixture.

The furnishings can be adult-size. Framed, permanent pictures, or durable frames with pictures to be changed at intervals are desirable.

Teaching materials include, in addition to the quarterlies, workbooks and special kits, a Bible for each pupil, globe of the world, maps, screen, and flannelgraph equipment.

SENIOR HIGH:

The classroom should accommodate twenty-five pupils, with twelve to fifteen square feet per pupil. It ought to be separate from the rest of the school. The chalkboard is to be clean and ready for use.

The furnishings are the usual tables and chairs, now adult size, framed pictures, and the inevitable wastebasket and offering receptacle.

Teaching materials for the Senior High classroom are the customary quarterlies or textbooks, Bibles, maps, flannelgraph, and perhaps a picture screen.

ADULTS and OLDER YOUNG PEOPLE:

The classroom is to be individual, if possible, with a class of twenty-five pupils. Eight to twelve square feet per pupil is considered good, under eight square feet, poor. Often an outline is placed on the wall chalkboard before the class begins.

The furnishings still should be table and chairs, or table-arm chairs, although lapboards can be used by pupils when rooms are crowded. Pictures are desirable, but keep them Christian. How about flags?

Teaching materials include the usual quarterlies or textbooks, Bibles, paper and pencils, maps, flannelgraph (yes, this is now used for young people and adults), picture screen, and perhaps other visual aids.

ADMINISTRATION ROOM OR OFFICE:

This room should be especially equipped with a superintendent's desk and cabinet as well as desks and cabinets for the various secretaries and treasurer. Particularly do the secretaries need desk and cabinet space, secluded from the other parts of the school.

The literature librarian can do his work in the church's library and equipment room if necessary, but it would be well if his table and cabinet were in the same room with the other officers.

ADDITIONAL INFORMATION:

Fixtures, furnishings, and teaching materials are steadily increasing in quantity and improving in quality. As superintendent, you will need to be well informed about them. The catalogs from the church publishing house, your local bookstore, and the public-school purchasing agent are the best sources of information.

Have you ever visited a school supply store or seen a catalog of equipment for the public schools? One superintendent, when he saw such a catalog, exclaimed, "I never knew such things existed!" Your school's librarian, or purchasing agent, ought to study the catalogs with you so that you can both become familiar with teaching aids.

The smallest and largest Sunday schools alike need stock rooms and libraries. One person, a member of the superintendent's staff, can manage both. But it must be the right person.

The stock room may be a cabinet or an entire room. In it are the general supplies from which the teachers and other workers draw. These supplies cost money, the Lord's money, for which you, as superintendent, are responsible. They include a multitude of things, all the way from pencils and paper to portable chalkboards, maps, projectors, filmstrips and slides, paste, scissors, etc. The person in charge may be one of the staff secretaries, the purchasing agent, librarian, or another responsible person. To repeat, this person is important. He must keep records, be able to operate and tell others how to operate the equipment, be able to repair equipment. More than that, he must be tactful as well as thorough in looking after the school's interests. If a teacher borrows equipment, he is to see that it is promptly returned after use and carefully operated or conserved while in use.

There is a danger that an equipment custodian may act as though the supplies are his own private, personal property, and thus discourage their use. Instead, he should be a salesman, encouraging the teachers to use the equipment, and taking pride in the successful use of the materials placed under his charge.

The library for the Sunday school, or for the church as a whole, is not to take the place of the public library. Books of fiction, unless they are Christian stories for some particular purpose, and other books of a general nature can be found in better supply in almost every community library. The church library should include books for the particular use of the church, such as Bible dictionaries, commentaries, concordances, books on superintending and teaching in the Sunday school, general books on Christian education, seasonal program books, departmental books for teachers and workers, etc.

The librarian is to keep careful records of all books purchased and of their use. He will look upon the books as agents to help in the training of workers and to help teach the Bible. He will keep himself informed regarding the new books available, and will lead the church in setting up a plan to purchase books regularly. He will keep the books, magazines, and papers neat and mended, ready for use. He will see that they are put to use, and do not merely collect dust on the shelves. The success of the library depends on this person. If he is one who realizes that teachers and other workers must continually read books to help them with their work, and that such reading is necessary to progress, the library will succeed under his direction.

Sometimes a church librarian can co-operate with a local Bible bookstore, or with the publishers, by taking orders for new books of general interests, books for gifts, Bibles and similar items that church members want but do not know how to obtain. Such bookstores and publishing houses will in turn provide the librarian with brochures on new books and catalogs to help him keep informed concerning available books and literature.

YOU SUPERVISE

TAKE AN INVENTORY

Now that we know what equipment is needed for a good Sunday school, suppose we take an inventory of your school. Following is a suggested inventory blank, which can be mimeographed. Give a copy to each teacher to be filled out and returned to you.

Class _____

Teacher _____

A. ROOM

Size: _____ feet by _____ feet

Number of pupils in class _____

Light: windows _____ size _____

        artificial _____

Heat: type _____; adequate? _____

Ventilation: summer _____

               winter _____

Good features:

Bad features:

Improvements needed:

B. EQUIPMENT

Tables: height _____; kind _____

Chairs: height _____; kind _____

Tackboard, size _____

Chalkboard, size _____

Supply cupboard _____

Wall pictures (list) _____

Visual aids (list) _____

Good features:

Bad features:

Improvements needed:

C. TEACHING MATERIALS (check ones used)

Quarterlies: teacher _____; pupil _____

Workbooks _____

Handwork _____

Pictures _____

Bibles _____

Maps _____

Visual aids _____

Good features:

Bad features:

Improvements needed:

Making this inventory is a good way to begin your school's program of improving its equipment. Learn what improvements are needed in each class. Make a list of them. Discuss them with the departmental superintendents and the board of Christian education. Begin now to make your school's equipment such as will teach that God is truly the owner of all that is, and that the church building is the place in which people worship Him and study His Word.

Can you give two reasons for taking up an offering in the Sunday-school hour? After you have read this page, you will know these reasons.

What three basic plans are used for financing the Sunday school? Which of these plans is the most common? Why? Read page 133 for the answers.

Why is an envelope system good in the Sunday school as well as in the worship services of the church? Page 133 tells you the reasons.

Can you name three things that must be considered before making out a yearly budget? Who is responsible for outlining the Sunday-school budget? Read page 134.

CHAPTER 17

YOU SUPERVISE

financing

Your Sunday school takes up offerings for two reasons: first, to train in Christian stewardship; second, to help pay its expenses.

Giving is a part of Christian worship. The Lord gave himself for us. We give in order to glorify Him. This giving is emphasized so much in the New Testament that some people hold it to be almost an ordinance of the church, like baptism and the Lord's Supper. The school teaches its pupils to worship. Therefore, it takes up an offering.

It teaches that the chief reason for our giving is to worship the Lord and that the Christian gives during the worship service of the church. This seems to be an understanding in most congregations and explains why one offering is taken in the school and another, the chief offering, is taken during the formal worship service.

Besides teaching the pupils how to worship, taking up offerings in the Sunday school helps to pay the expenses of the school. Few schools, however, are self-supporting. They depend on the general church treasury for the building, light, heat, and other expenses. They pay for their own immediate expenses but expect the church's membership to provide the accommodations. This is as it should be. It is little enough for the church to provide the accommodations for the Sunday school.

Members of the Sunday school ought to be told where their money goes. They should realize that it costs money to provide and maintain the school, and that lesson materials and other supplies cost money. Their offerings help to pay the bills. They ought to be told it is the Lord's work to which their money is given. The Lord said,

"Go . . . teach." Their offerings help carry out this great commission. In the children's departments the offering is usually a devotional experience, the little ones learning the importance of giving to God's work.

HOW TO TAKE UP OFFERINGS

Three radically different plans are used for financing the Sunday school:

1. The most common method is to take up an offering in each class or department each Sunday morning and turn it in to the school's secretary. She makes a record of the amount and gives the money to the treasurer. The treasurer, then, is responsible for paying the bills of the Sunday school.

2. For some years the more professional Christian educators have been arguing for a single church treasury, to which money is given by the church members and used for all purposes, including the Sunday school. Under this method an offering may or may not be taken up in the Sunday school.

3. The third, and least common plan, is for the Sunday school to take the lead in paying for all the work of the church. One church in Texas has a yearly budget of $50,000, $44,000 of which comes through the Sunday school.

If the offering is to be taken in the school for the support of the school (this seems to be the accepted method in most schools at this time), it should be done systematically. This suggests the envelope plan. (See the discussion of the six-point plan in chapter 14.) This is an excellent way to teach the pupil to give "upon the first day of the week" and "as God hath prospered him."

If the six-point-plan envelopes are given to the pupils ahead of time, for three, six, or even twelve months, they can be taught to give regularly, whether they are present at Sunday school or not. Some schools use a special duplex offering envelope for Sunday school, similar to that used in the worship services. The use of such envelopes has been known to increase the offerings as much as four times.

This systematic, instructive method of encouraging offerings in the Sunday school does not lower the giving for general church purposes. On the contrary, the usual testimony is that such means of encouraging giving in the Sunday school invariably increases the giving in the worship services. The superintendent may be assured, therefore, that emphasis on giving in the Sunday school will not reduce the giving of the church members.

BE CAREFUL! YOU ARE USING GOD'S MONEY

You, the superintendent, are responsible for seeing that the money received from the pupils of the Sunday school is carefully accounted for and carefully spent. Careful accounting begins with the departmental or class secretary or treasurer who notes the amount of the offering in the classbook or on the class envelope. The school's secretary then enters this amount on the record and adds up the class offerings to find the total offering. This total is then recorded. The secretary must check the amount recorded for each class, counting it to make sure that the class record is correct. The total offering is turned over to the school's treasurer (or to the church's treasurer).

The board of Christian education authorizes how the money is to be spent. Some of this authorization is general, as in the case of the regular quarterly lesson supplies and papers. Other spending must be authorized specifically, such as for a Sunday-school picnic. Under no circumstances will a wise superintendent assume the responsibility for expenditures. He will insist that they be authorized by the proper parties, that the authorization be entered in the secretary's record, and payment made according to official procedure. This method protects everyone against suspicion of carelessness or dishonesty.

At least once each year the books are audited. This too, is for the protection of the superintendent, secretary, treasurer, etc. The auditing committee's report is made a part of the record. Usually, the church as a whole names an auditing committee or employs a professional auditor to make the annual check of the record books.

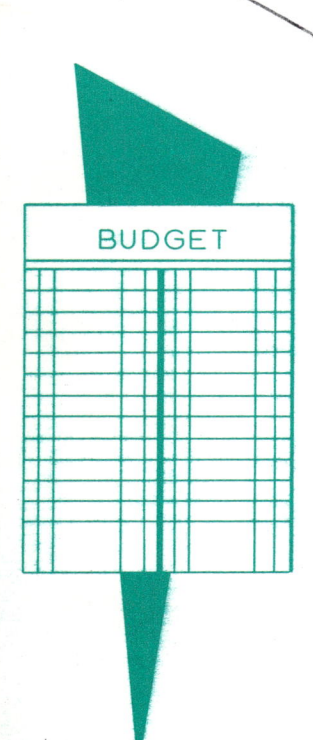

THE BUDGET

Expenditures are to be made as provided by the school's annual budget. This budget is prepared by the superintendent, treasurer, and others who may be designated to do the work. It is then submitted to the board of education and to the workers' conference for discussion. It may be adopted by them, or adopted by the entire congregation at its annual meeting. The budget is for a year's expenditures and is adopted prior to the beginning of the school year.

Three things must be taken into consideration as you prepare the school's budget:
1. The school's requirements (what is needed).
2. Records of expenditures of former years.
3. The rate at which the school is growing and the number of prospective projects listed in the school's plan for the coming year.

After these things are considered, see how the results compare with the estimated income for the year. It may be necessary to adjust the budget to keep the expenditures within the expected income. Some items may have to be reduced, others dropped entirely. The superintendent will lead in making the necessary adjustment.

Now comes the job of raising the money to meet the budget. This is a week-by-week procedure. The superintendent will give careful attention to see that the income is keeping pace with the expenditures. The treasurer's report at each meeting of the workers' conference will keep the workers advised on this point.

On the following page is a typical budget, taken from the actual records of a large Sunday school that has followed the budget plan for many years. Notice, we said *typical* budget—not *recommended* budget. No two schools are alike. Each school must estimate its own needs and its own income, and then prepare its own budget based on its findings.

A TYPICAL SUNDAY-SCHOOL BUDGET

1. *Literature.* Lesson periodicals and other materials that come regularly for classroom use. — $1800.00

2. *Printing and Mailing.* Publicity and greeting cards. — 100.00

3. *Supplies.* Crayons, pencils, paper, paste, and other items needed by teachers. — 75.00

4. *Relief.* To care for needy children and homes. This is an emergency fund, administered by a special committee, with authority to act. — 150.00

5. *Athletics.* Rental of gymnasium, purchase of equipment for basketball and baseball teams, etc. — 200.00

6. *Youth.* Banquet for school graduates; refreshments for youth gatherings. — 100.00

7. *Vacation Bible School.* This is only a part of these expenses, and goes mostly to provide transportation. — 225.00

8. *Special Days.* Decorations, tags, promotion, motion pictures taken for school's historical file, awards such as flowers on Mother's Day, promotion certificates, treats for children. — 250.00

9. *Picnic.* Rental of grounds, treats, prizes. — 135.00

10. *Bus.* The church provides a bus for the purpose of bringing pupils to and from Sunday school. — 400.00

11. *Teacher Training.* Library, filmstrips, expense of institutes and workshops. — 75.00

12. *Equipment.* Permanent equipment such as filmstrips, slides, projectors, chalkboards, flannelboards, draperies. — 150.00

13. *Weekly Bulletin.* The church publishes and distributes to all members a weekly paper and the school pays its share of the cost. — 200.00

14. *Cleaning.* Linen for nursery and restrooms; care and repair of furnishings and equipment. — 100.00

15. *Building Fund.* This is a "cushion" item, to absorb any money remaining after the expenses of the school are paid. — 400.00

TOTAL $4360.00
PER WEEK 83.84

Section 5

you analyze

Chapter 18—Results

Worksheets:
    You Visualize
    You Organize
    You Deputize
    You Supervise

Do you know how often (at least) you should stop to take stock of your school—to find out if it is successful and what improvements should be made? Read this page for the answer.

How can this chapter help you to analyze your school's improvements and progress? Read pages 138 and 139. Then use the work sheets on pages 140 and 143.

Can you name five suggestions that are given to help you use the work sheets or charts? They are given for you on pages 138 and 139.

Remember—do not become discouraged in your work as superintendent. Use the work sheets in this chapter as guides for more detailed charts to be given to your teachers and officers so they can measure their improvements also.

CHAPTER 18

YOU ANALYZE

results

If you are a successful superintendent your school will improve. To help bring about this improvement, you need to pause at least once every month and take stock of your school's situation. A good time to do this is just before the monthly conference of officers and teachers, so that you can discover any weaknesses in the school's program and be prepared to make recommendations to correct these weaknesses.

Your program of progress will involve the proper visualizing of your school's importance and purpose, its organization, the deputizing of responsible workers, and supervision of all activities connected with the school. In other words, it will involve the topics and suggestions included in this book.

For each of the four preceding sections of this book there is provided an analysis work sheet or chart to help you measure your Sunday school's progress. Here are five suggestions to help you use these charts:

1. After you have read the seventeen preceding chapters in this book, make a list of improvements you believe your school should make in connection with each chapter heading.

2. Discuss these improvements with your officers and teachers so thoroughly that they will join you in wanting to see the improvements made.

3. Set up a time schedule. All of the improvements cannot be made immediately. Some may require considerable time. Others cannot be undertaken until preliminary steps are taken. The time schedule should

be flexible so that it can be adjusted as you proceed. Every worker in the school must be familiar with the program of improvement and with the time set for the accomplishment of each undertaking.

4. You may wish to prepare more detailed work sheets for your staff of officers and teachers so that they can check their progress from time to time. The work sheets printed here are mainly for your own use in evaluating the improvement of your school under your leadership.

5. Do not become discouraged. Your school will never be perfect, just as the individual people in the school will never be perfect while on this earth. But you can strive for perfection and keep trying to make your Sunday school better and better. Remember, you are not working alone in this effort. You have a divine "general superintendent." He is also your Chief, Master, King, and Lord—Jesus Christ. He will help you. Consult Him often. Depend upon Him always, and lead your workers to depend on Him also, while they, along with you, strive diligently to do their part.

On the next four pages are the analysis work sheets—one for each preceding section in this book. You are to change the work sheets in any way you wish to make them fit your particular needs and situation. Beneath each chart, and on page 144, space is provided so that you can make necessary notes.

WORK SHEET I

Section 1—YOU VISUALIZE	Stage of Progress*				
	1	2	3	4	5
My school's officers, teachers, and I can explain convincingly why our school is important.					
We understand fully, and can explain to others, the twofold purpose of the Sunday school.					
Our school is fulfilling its purpose of recruiting people to Christ as it should be.					
The Sunday school of which I am superintendent is fulfilling its purpose of conserving Christians.					
Our school is keeping pace with the population growth in our community.					

* Use this work sheet to measure your progress in improving your school. When an improvement is first begun, make a check mark in column 1. As improvements progress, check under columns 2, 3, and 4. When the improvement is completed, make a final check mark under column 5.

NOTES

WORK SHEET II

Section 2—YOU ORGANIZE	Stage of Progress*				
	1	2	3	4	5
My fellow workers can explain what the church is, know who is its head, and what it does. (Chapter 2)					
My staff and I co-operate with the board of Christian education and minister and understand fully the other teaching activities of the church. (Chapter 2)					
Our school is organized with a superintendent over each department or division. (Chapter 3)					
Each department has its own staff of officers and teachers who report to the departmental superintendent. (Chapter 3)					
The lessons, equipment, and program in each class is graded to accommodate the pupils in that class. (Chapter 3)					
I know the advantages and disadvantages of the four types of lesson materials and know which type is best for each class in our school. (Chapter 4)					
We have a definite method of encouraging teachers to make the best use of their teaching material. (Chapter 4)					
Our Sunday school has an annual program that is tied in with the year's program for the entire church. (Chapter 5)					
We have a program committee that provides a variety of interesting Sunday morning programs for our school. (Chapter 5)					

* Use this work sheet to measure your progress in improving your school. When an improvement is first begun, make a check mark in column 1. As improvements progress, check under columns 2, 3, and 4. When the improvement is completed, make a final check mark under column 5.

NOTES

WORK SHEET III

Section 3—YOU DEPUTIZE	Stage of Progress*				
	1	2	3	4	5
I know four good reasons why I should never do anything that I can enlist someone else to do. (Chapter 6)					
Our school has a definite plan for discovering, training, and enlisting every member of the church as a worker for the Lord. (Chapter 6)					
Every officer in our school meets the qualifications listed in chapter 7.					
Each officer is chosen for one year only and is replaced when he is no longer the best available person for the job. (Chapter 7)					
Our teachers are selected annually by the church's board of Christian education. (Chapter 8)					
Every teacher in our school is constantly striving to improve in ability; each one is honest, a teamworker, and actively participates in the entire program of the church. (Chapter 8)					
Our board of Christian education sees to it that every worker is given pre-service and in-service training. (Chapter 10)					

* Use this work sheet to measure your progress in improving your school. When an improvement is first begun, make a check mark in column 1. As improvements progress, check under columns 2, 3, and 4. When the improvement is completed, make a final check mark under column 5.

NOTES

YOU ANALYZE

WORK SHEET IV

Section 4—YOU SUPERVISE	Stage of Progress*				
	1	2	3	4	5
I have listed my spiritual weaknesses and have taken the necessary steps to eliminate them. (Chapter 11)					
I am physically fit to serve as superintendent of the Sunday school according to the recommendations in chapter 11.					
I personally supervise the officers of my school; each understands his duties clearly. (Chapter 12)					
The teachers are directly supervised by their departmental superintendents; the departmental superintendents come to me with teacher problems when my help is needed. (Chapter 12)					
Our school holds regular workers' conferences (at least once a month) for the entire staff of teachers and officers. (Chapter 13)					
Our workers' conferences include the seven essential factors described in chapter 13.					
I indirectly supervise the pupils in our school through the teachers; we successfully use the six-point plan. (Chapter 14)					
Our school complies fully with the rules for attendance building as outlined in chapter 15.					
The housekeeping, arrangement, lighting, heat, ventilation, etc., in our classrooms are all that could be desired according to the requirements given in chapter 16.					
The furnishings, as described in chapter 16, are as nearly ideal for every class as we can make them; we have plans for improving them.					
Every officer, teacher, and pupil in our school understands clearly why offerings are received. (Chapter 17)					
Careful records are kept of the offerings in each class, department, and in the entire school; the money is spent wisely and carefully, and records are kept of all expenditures. (Chapter 17)					

*Use this work sheet to measure your progress in improving your school. When an improvement is first begun, make a check mark in column 1. As improvements progress, check under columns 2, 3, and 4. When the improvement is completed, make a final check mark under column 5.

NOTES